MW01121986

DATE DUE	RETURNED

Life Without Death

The Cinema of Frank Cole

Edited by Mike Hoolboom and Tom McSorley

Canadian Film Institute

This book was made possible through generous funding by the Canadian Film Institute, the AV Trust and the Canada Council for the Arts. The editors are very grateful for this support.

Every effort has been made to contact copyright holders of images and text; please notify the Canadian Film Institute if we have made an error or omission and we will correct it in subsequent editions.

LIBRARY AND ARCHIVES CANADA CATALOGUING IN PUBLICATION

Life without death : the cinema of Frank Cole / editors: Mike Hoolboom, Tom McSorley.

ISBN 978-0-919096-43-1

1. Cole, Frank--Criticism and interpretation. 2. Cole, Frank. 3. Motion picture producers and directors--Canada--Biography. I. Hoolboom, Michael II. McSorley, Tom III. Canadian Film Institute IV. Title.

PN1998.3.C6659L53 2009   791.4302'33092   C2009-901574-9

Contents

All Franked Out
Mike Hoolboom and Tom McSorley

They told him not to go and he went. They said it was impossible and he climbed up over that too. The limit, the stop sign, the forbidden; he called all that home.

When we talked to one notable wag about contributing to this volume, he begged off. He just couldn't anymore. He'd spent the long nights after Frank's death talking to friends and family and those who knew him least of all at conferences and festivals and gatherings and now he was at the end of his frankness. His frankability. Not one more word, please. He said he was "all Franked out."

Frank Cole is a long trip. While he managed to complete only four movies, each is filled with a blood commitment that is more usually resolved in sacraments of marriage or death. And for all their stern, visionary rigour, they remain home movies, family snaps that never wander far from the side of his grandfather, who dies slowly over the course of each film, again and again. Frank's cinema is a wound that never stops opening, beautiful and terrible in equal measures. To survive these pictures, he reschooled himself, applying the strictest codes of discipline. He left possessions behind and withdrew into solitude. He took up weightlifting and an obsessive diet that found him portioning out his grief in calories, and then in pictures. He knew better than anyone that these movies had to be lived before they could be introduced to the camera.

Is it strange to welcome a book about a man who regarded language as a foreign country?

When he talked, the words would begin somewhere deep inside the body, where cells were busy dividing and forming new lines of tissue and filament. It came through miles of intestine and bloodlines and emerged in a slow-motion deadpan. How. Are. You. He spoke as if each word were its own sentence, and even when he was repeating tried-and-truisms, he laid them out as if language were discovering itself for the first time. He was a stranger to small talk and easy party chatter. The restless flow of language, where meaning could be found in the flux, carried away by its own relentless tide, all this was strange to him. He might have learned to speak listening to his diplomat father, who took him around the world one carefully parsed line at a time, the diction groomed in policy documents and terse encounters with states in transition. During the invasion that ended the Czech spring, for instance, or the apartheid regime in South Africa, the conflicts between India and Pakistan. If Frank's words were forged during wartime, their economy ensured that they were already a form of writing.

This experience of the chaos of martial reality and its vocabularies of uncertainty, displacement, dispossession, and death clearly mark Frank's work, on the screen and on the page. The paradoxes of such lived experiences are embodied in his œuvre: a taut aesthetic cinematic code and a life reduced to monkish asceticism to explore the vicissitudes of living, dying, solitude, losing loved ones. There is, in this compelling work, a lean musculature sculpted by the profound tensions between infinity and closure, between definite and indefinite, between reduction and irreducibility: in life and in cinema. This is an artist, in so many senses, at war, and the war is fought on the daunting, elusive fronts of memory, epistemology, the body, and time itself.

This volume collects voices near and far. His family is here, along with friends and familiars, and of course there are his own words, precious words, sounded out in interviews or excerpted from a book-length volume composed at the end of long days during his Sahara treks. But there are also others who weigh in for whom Frank was only a distant rumour, or an unnoticed glimmer in cinema's infinite rectangle. Many are artists, or programmers who shape their public lighting like artists, or critics who have occupied parallel territories. All have been encouraged to speak in the first person, to allow their own hopes to rub up against his unreasonable emulsions. These multiple openings offer viewing platforms that can be tested, argued, tried. They bring local knowledge to Cole's tightly enclosed infinities. Benjamin writes that there are two kinds of storytellers: the ones who stay rooted and learn the lore of their habitat, and the others who carry stories from one place to another. Frank was both, of course, sometimes at the same time, so perhaps it's no surprise that this volume collects nomads and recluses, believers and skeptics, desert travellers and artists whose real worlds begin with the opening of a book. Let a thousand Franks flourish.

Perhaps Frank Cole sought death; not as some gesture of quixotic and romantic heroism, but as an intensely curious displaced person, a nomad in a world he understood to be, metaphorically at least, a desert of constant flux, its sands shifting in continual contigency. One thing seems clear: death spoke to Frank Cole and he bravely formulated a response. The dialogues collected here attempt, with varying degrees of risk and candour, to honour his modest, doomed, and indefatigable answer to whatever questions he may have heard emanating from his grandfather's small hospital bed or from those ancient restless plains of the Sahara.

This publication accompanies a tour of Frank's work, and soon there will be handsome new DVDs available. It's our hope that you will be able to see his charmed pictures for yourself, and invent the new and necessary pleasures that might yet accompany each of us while walking across our own Saharas.

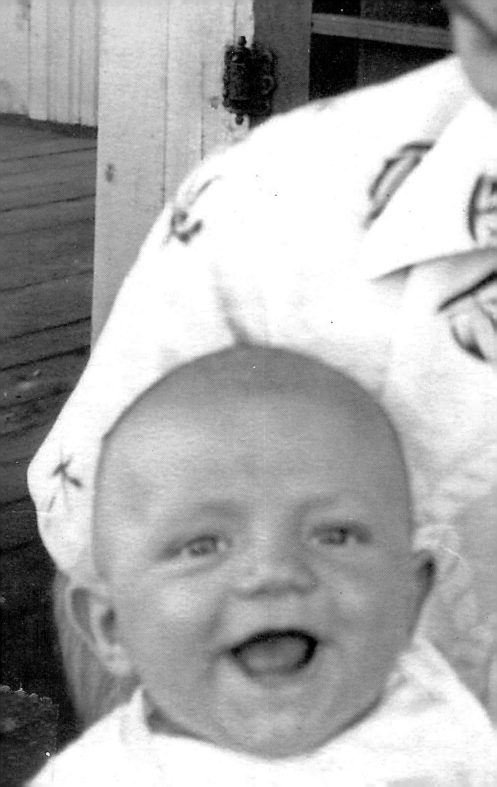

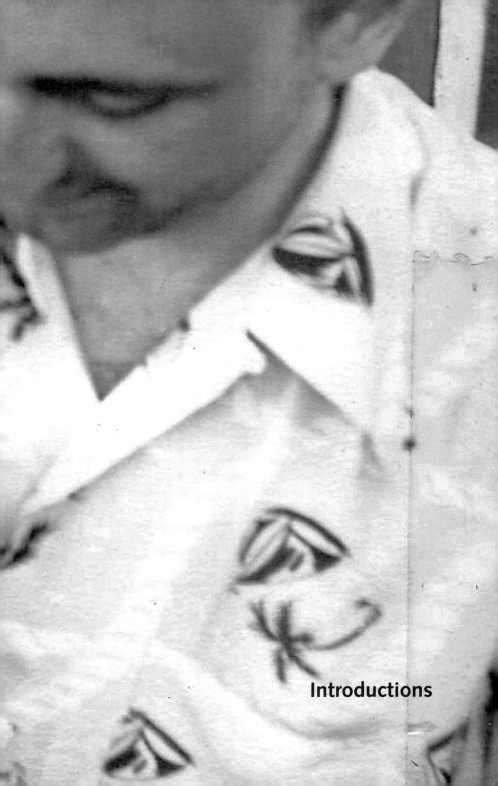

Introductions

Life During Wartime
An Interview with Charles Cole by Korbett Matthews

CHARLES COLE: My wife, Jean, was born in Saskatchewan, and I went out there in 1950 to teach law. Frank was born on March 26, 1954, in Saskatoon, and a year later we moved to Ottawa when I got a job with External Affairs. Frank was about five years old when he began to wait outside the front door of our home for my return from work. When the new season commenced, he was reluctant to come inside until we agreed that he could help clean the driveway after dinner. In those days we did not have a snow blower, but used shovels, including a small one for Frank. It was not long before he became frustrated at not being able to clean the snow off right down to the asphalt. As he grew older, he was gradually able to accomplish this objective. In later years, when he had his own apartment, he offered to come and help me with the snow. Although we had a snow blower, he was not satisfied until the snow was removed right down to the asphalt, which usually meant using a shovel.

We still live in Ottawa, though we had five postings in the following years, the first one in Pakistan. We were located in Karachi for about a year, and we enjoyed our time there, particularly on Sundays when we went out to the beach near the Arabian Sea. That was where Frank had his first camel ride. The local people would come along with camels and Frank wanted to have a ride. You can see a photo of that ride in his film *Life Without Death*. He was nine years old. This experience must have lodged in his mind all the following years.

We then moved to Rawalpindi in northwestern Pakistan, where the High Commission in Karachi had opened an office adjacent to the new capital of Islamabad. We had taken our small chihuahua with us to Pakistan, which was a mistake. Frank was very attached to that dog and in the summer of 1964, our first summer in Rawalpindi, the dog became ill. There were no veterinarians available. The Pakistani army doctors tried to help out but they were accustomed to treating horses. As a result, our chihuahua died and Frank was heartbroken. This was his first encounter with death.

During the hostilities between India and Pakistan in 1965, all the Western children except Frank were withdrawn. Their parents had arranged for them to leave the country, and the Americans took a number of them out on their flight. Rawalpindi had been bombed in the late evening and early morning of September 6, 1965. While serious damage had not been done, it raised concern that there might be further bombing if the ceasefire did not hold. Frank came into my office and asked me to come out to the garden, and I was quite puzzled why. Gardens are nice, but when you have work to do, you can always look at the gardens later. But I went with him, and he said that when Rawalpindi is bombed again, here is a place I could seek shelter. He showed me a trench he had dug, and said that a Pakistani friend had helped him with the digging. It showed great persistence for an eleven-year-old, and I think that was typical of Frank. He was always considerate.

On August 21, 1968, the invasion of Czechoslovakia took place. I got a call from a Czechoslovakian who spoke English quite well. He said, "Mr. Cole, Mr. Cole, they're here!" He was crying. This was shortly after two in the morning, so I thanked him for letting me know. It was a great surprise for me, as it was to many others in Czechoslovakia. I woke Jean and Frank and told them that I had to go to the embassy and that they should come with me. I asked them to dress warmly and to take good walking shoes because we didn't know what we were facing. Frank turned up at the front door with his tennis gear and rackets all set to go. I was in charge of the embassy until the arrival of an ambassador five months later and arranged for an office driver to come pick us up. I told him that if it was dangerous he shouldn't come. But he turned up and we got in the car and drove down the wide thoroughfare of Leninova, and every few yards there was a tank. There were no other cars visible. None of us said a word when we drove between the tanks, which formed a long column into the horizon. I thought: It's just going to take one shell from one of those tanks and the family will be wiped out, including the driver. As far as the Coles are concerned, we all go at the same time. In its own way, that was a bit comforting.

Frank never talked much about his feelings during the invasion of Czechoslovakia, but it undoubtedly had a major influence on his thinking. I regret that my work made it difficult to spend much time with him.

I was particularly concerned that I might be prevented from returning to the embassy during the early stages of the occupation when there was so much to be done. An immediate priority was providing assistance to the many Canadians (including scientists and family members) attending the World Geological Congress in Prague who were stranded by the cancellation of air flights, trains and buses. There was much relief when surface transportation resumed within a few days.

During long days and some nights, I remained at the embassy with a few staff members. Shortly after the occupation an 8 p.m. curfew had been announced, which resulted in empty streets and risky travel. Although there were plenty of worries, I was somewhat reassured that Frank was at home with his mother, Jean, even though a large group of the invaders had set up camp in the beautiful park across the street from our house. In early September, the embassy in Vienna asked if we could assist a Canadian air stewardess whose three-year-old daughter was visiting her Czechoslovak grandparents. Could we get her to Vienna? As Jean would be accompanying Frank to school in Switzerland in a few days via Vienna, she volunteered to help out. It was not an easy trip. They were disturbed several times during the night by Soviet soldiers knocking on their compartment door and demanding entry. Jean credits Frank for the satisfactory resolution of this problem and the reunion of the little girl with her mother.

Frank went to school in Pakistan from 1963 to 1965, he was back in Ottawa in 1965 to 1968, and from 1968 to 1971 he was at school in Switzerland. He was schooled in South Africa in 1971 and for a brief period in 1972 and then went

back to Switzerland to complete his matriculation there. He had a great variety of schooling and never said much about it, but I think all these adjustments were hard on him. In South Africa, he attended school in Cape Town, and the arrangement at that time was that the Canadian embassy spent roughly six months in Cape Town and six months in the administrative capital of Pretoria. Frank did not react very well to school in South Africa. I couldn't understand at first why he was unhappy, but apartheid was still very much a factor in daily life in South Africa at that time. And school discipline didn't go down with him very well. Minor infractions could result in heavy reprisals and Frank could have weathered that, but he didn't like the principle of it.

One morning at roughly three o'clock I received a telephone call from the school in Cape Town and was told that Frank had disappeared. Needless to say, this was quite shocking to me. It was the middle of the night and here was Frank wandering around. So I quickly dressed and thought about where he might possibly be. I didn't inform the police that he was missing, but went looking for him myself and wondered where a sixteen-year-old unhappy boy might be at that time of the morning. I drove out to the airport and sat in the lounge from 4:30 to 9. It was a long wait. Around 9, who should walk into the lounge but

Frank. I was so relieved. I asked him to come to Pretoria, where our present home was, and in the meantime to stay with me in the hotel. I could see that the best place for him was to go back to Switzerland, where he had been very happy, and that's what he did. But for the first time I really understood how determined he was. When he made a decision, it was almost impossible to change his mind. I think that this personality trait undoubtedly had to do with his obsession about the Sahara. He told me once that he was never happier than when he was in the Sahara, despite all the challenges and dangers.

When we were posted in South Africa, the embassy was located in Cape Town, the legislative capital. We rented a house and hired a housekeeper who had worked for the owner. Her name was Minnie and we were delighted with

her services. In 1971 we were transferred to Pretoria, where Frank would join us at the end of his school year. We had maintained contact with Minnie and invited her to visit us. It would be her first trip away from Cape Town. We arranged a ticket with South African Airways and for Frank to accompany her. She had never travelled by air. As things turned out, Frank's schoolmate, the son of an American diplomat, would be taking the same flight. When boarding the aircraft, Minnie was told to take a seat at the rear, while Frank and his friend were shown seats at the front. Contrary to apartheid regulations, Frank and his friend moved to the rear to sit with Minnie during the two-hour flight. The embassy never heard anything about this incident from the South African authorities.

When we returned from South Africa to Ottawa in 1972, Frank played a lot of tennis at the club and then started engaging in competitions. He and another player won the Canadian doubles championship in 1972 in Vancouver, if my memory serves me correctly. He started attending Carleton University that fall and completed his BA degree.

At that time we had been posted to Holland while he remained in Canada. We were separated from Frank for long periods of time on postings, and Jean's parents became substitutes for us. Particularly Jean's father. You can see that from his films. Frank was so solicitous, so helpful to Jean's father, and Jean's father was very important to his development.

The next thing we knew he had enrolled in a filmmaking course at Algonquin College. He spent three years there, and that's where he learned his craft.

KORBETT MATTHEWS: Where do you think Frank's obsession about the Sahara came from? What made him want to travel across such inhospitable lands?

CC: I think he wanted to show that he could do it. And he wanted to show *himself* that he could do it. I could be wrong; I always respected Frank's privacy and inner thoughts and would rarely question him too much. He seemed to be able to look after himself so well. There was little I could do to influence any decisions.

When I picked him up on his return from the Sahara, I believe it was in November 1990, he was the last one to come through customs and immigration from the Mirabel Airport, and I wondered what was delaying him. Finally, some minutes after the last person except Frank had come through, I saw him walk through the doors carrying what looked like a saddle. And sure enough, that's what it was. He said he'd been delayed because the customs people had become fascinated by the saddle and wished to talk to him. They seemed to be very interested in where he had been and so on. On the drive back to Ottawa, I said to Frank that I hoped he had some better clothes because the clothing he was wearing, even his jeans, were pretty worn out. Frank replied, "Dad, these are the best clothes I have." I gathered later that he had worn the same pair of black Levi's during the entire trip.

On the drive back from the airport he told me that he was thinking about going into medicine. I said, "That's quite a change, isn't it? Why would you want to do that? You should have started years before." He said, "Well, Dad, when I was in Chad waiting for permission to go to the Sudan, I helped a German doctor who was trying to cope with many people who needed medical attention." He added, "I'm thinking that's something I might do, to go back to the Sahara and try to help people."

KM: When did he tell you he wanted to return to the desert?

CC: That same evening. I said to him, "Well, Frank, I suppose you've had enough of the Sahara now," and that I'd be glad to see him back in Canada for a while. He said, "Dad, I'm already planning my next trip to the Sahara." What could I say? Frank was very systematic. I believe he intended to make regular trips back to the Sahara, working on his films in the meantime.

KM: Did he speak to you about what happened on his first journey?

CC: No, he didn't. There are a lot of things I don't know. He kept a lot of detailed notes about his trip across the Sahara and worked on a book based on these notes. They answer some questions but it's very difficult for me to say definitely, "This is what he thought." I asked him once if he was ever afraid on this trip of almost a year. He said, "Dad, there was never a minute I wasn't afraid." He was afraid of running out of water or being robbed, or sustaining an injury that would not permit him to continue. He didn't articulate all this to me, but I understood. He was determined to complete it nonetheless. One thing I know about Frank is that when he made up his mind to do something, he would do it.

There's only one thing I know of that he would have liked to have done but refused, and this shows some flexibility. He wouldn't do anything that would deliberately endanger his own life; that is, he wouldn't do anything that would certainly run the risk of death. When he was in Peru, he used to go to the beach and stay out there and surf. He loved surfing. With great patience, he taught his younger brother Peter to surf that afternoon after many tumbles. I thought he was too young to begin to surf, but Frank persisted and won the struggle.

In 1984, Jean and I were posted to Peru, where I took charge of the embassy's consular section. This involved regular visits to Canadians imprisoned for drug trafficking in Peru and Bolivia. On my first visit to La Paz, the capital

of Bolivia, I was recognized by one of the prisoners who had played tennis with Frank many times as teenagers. When Frank visited us some months later in Lima, I mentioned this meeting. He was eager to know how his friend was faring. I told him he was nearing the end of his twelve-year sentence, but serious depression was obviously a factor, caused mainly by the prevailing conditions. These included the poor food, the absence of sanitation and the lack of basic comforts of life in a prison situated at an elevation of some 10,000 feet. Friendship with two other Canadian prisoners with whom he shared a gloomy cell seemed to be one of the few positive features.

Frank left Lima by bus a few days later on a sightseeing tour to Chile, including its Atacama Desert. I learned only after his return that he had changed his itinerary to visit his friend in La Paz, not forgetting to bring along some of his favourite food.

In Peru we had been reading about a huge wave that came in to the beach every year or so where he liked to swim. Day after day he sat on that beach waiting for the wave to come. It did come, and when he came back from the beach I said, "Well, I understand they had that big wave up there." "Yes," he said, "but I didn't try it. I realized it was too much for me." Of course I was greatly relieved to realize that he had an appreciation that there was some limitation to what he could do.

In 1987, my youngest sister, Marcella, died in Florida, where she had been living for some years. She was an American, born in New York City, and a graduate from Columbia University. In 1987, she telephoned and told me that she was ill and asked if Frank could find time to come down and help her a bit. I phoned Frank and of course he agreed immediately. Frank went twice, and was planning a third trip. I heard him say to his brother Peter, "You've got to come with me, we have to keep Marcella alive." Peter agreed and the tickets were booked, but the day they were to leave, word came that Marcella had died. In the days when she was entering her final illness, she called to tell me how much help Frank had been to her. That's the kind of consideration he maintained for his aunt, whom he didn't know very well since she had been living elsewhere for many years.

KM: I wonder if you could tell me about your impressions of Frank's last film?

CC: I didn't see anything of the film until it was shown at the Hot Docs Festival in Toronto. I asked Frank a number of times how it was coming along. He never told me very much, but he indicated that both he and Francis Miquet were working very hard. When I saw the film in Toronto for the first time in

May 2000, I was practically glued to my seat. I now had an idea of what he had gone through.

At that time, he was already back in the Sahara, and I wish I had been able to exert more influence on him not to make that trip. He called me from the Sahara sometime in June. It was a brief telephone conversation. He had encountered serious drought on the route that he was following and found the wells were dry. That's about all we had time to exchange. I tried to phone him back and couldn't get through. I kept trying all afternoon and finally had to give it up. That was the last time I talked to Frank.

KM: How did you find out about Frank's death?

CC: About his murder? The way we were informed was done with a great deal of empathy and consideration. Jean and I had gone down to Chile to visit our son Peter in October 2000. Peter took us around the country a bit. When we returned to his house in Santiago in late October, it seems the Ottawa police had tried to contact us. I realized that something must have been wrong and went to the Canadian embassy the following day. A young officer there told me about Frank, and the embassy offered whatever help it could, such as arranging transportation back to Canada.

Because of the distance, few details were known. But it was acknowledged that Frank had been murdered, and all of his possessions had been taken from him, including his two camels. In February 2001 we arranged to obtain Frank's DNA from the RCMP. Frank had left specimens of his saliva in case anything happened to him. We tried to obtain DNA earlier, but due to inexperience, we were slow in getting it from other organizations that might have provided it. The remains were sent back by air to Detroit, where the Cryonics Institute is located. Frank was a member of that organization and had an agreement that his remains were to go there.

KM: Do you think the case will ever be solved?

CC: It's a hard question. We get hopeful signs from time to time from Mali, but it seems to be one step forward and two steps back. But we haven't given up. I don't believe in capital punishment, for one thing, and would never stand idly by if I knew some innocent person was being prosecuted. You saw from Frank's film the concern he evidenced when he thought the police might harm the man who stole his camel. Only time will tell what the final result will be.

The end of the world in
the usual dress

in a night full of hope.

Saltwater Road to the Sahara
Richard Taylor

Water brought Frank and I together one sunny afternoon at Ottawa's Carleton University in September 1972. Frank walked into my Spanish class in a surfing T-shirt with a thick, sun-bleached ponytail halfway down his back, and his fingers and both arms had braided elephant-hair rings and bracelets. Because he had just returned from living with his diplomat parents in Cape Town, South Africa, he'd been seduced by surfing. Wearing a blue SURFBOARDS HAWAII T-shirt, and a leather hippie headband around my blond shoulder-length hair, I was bronzed from two months surfing my ass off in Hawaii. With my headband, Frank's ponytail and our deep surfer tans, Frank and I looked like a couple of Hollywood Indians. I introduced myself. Always polite and focused, Frank stared right into my eyes and offered his hand to shake. "Hi, Rick, I'm Frank Cole, " he said. "Do you surf?" We were the only surfers in Ottawa. Fish out of water. It was love at first sight.

Along with a shared desire for balls-out surfing and swimming, I had the honour of becoming Frank's best friend. And along with this, the dubious honour of losing Frank Cole's first film.

A few years later, Frank was travelling in Europe with his girlfriend Jacinthe, shooting a surfing film along the coasts of Spain, Portugal and France. While my wife, Dale, and I travelled in a renovated hippie van for a year, surfing the perimeter of North America, Frank sent me letters about the joys of surfing with topless beauties in Biarritz. Then he posted a Super-8 film to us. That summer of 1976 he wrote: "Rick, I'm relieved the film reached you. It's my first film. I hope there are no technical problems with my shots, as the scenes in the film tend to be fleeting. It's a random series of impressions and reflections. Hang on to the film. Frank."

Because of a tip from Frank, toward the end of our year travelling in the van, Dale and I ended up surfing Sebastian Inlet in Florida. After an early-morning surf, we drove to Disneyworld and left our van in the Donald Duck parking lot. Unfortunately, at the end of the day, when we stepped off the shuttle bus at the parking lot, we discovered our van had been stolen. A brand-new surfboard, portable typewriter, my early manuscripts and Dale's wave paintings — everything we owned from a year of travelling had vanished, and was never recovered. Including Frank's first film.

"Travel is a vanishing act," Paul Theroux once wrote, "a solitary trip down a pinched line of geography to oblivion." As Frank used to say, even though it could swallow the United States, there is no exact map of the Sahara desert. When I first met him in Spanish class I didn't know we would embark on a deep friendship lasting twenty-eight years, one in which that desert would play a pivotal role — including becoming the site of his murder. Over the years, Frank said many times that I should write about him if something ever happened. So I kept a file of his cryptic postcards and letters from around the world. I have a thick sheaf of big letters and a wad of his very short postcards.

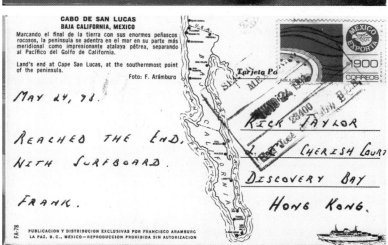

In many ways I've always been writing about Frank. He put an edge on my own obsession with various aspects of mortality. While he grew to confront death and dying head-on, I was a hopeless romantic who had to learn how to fight the seductive pull of melancholy. There's no avoiding death, so gradually over the years I discovered how to have fun and enjoy the ride.

Frank didn't just arrive here on earth ready to become a famous, desert-crossing filmmaker. His angst and desires evolved over time in tandem with me. Because we were both disconnected from the normal aspects of campus life, during our early years of university we gravitated more and more to one another. Our scholastic futures looked bleak until we discovered that we could find salvation if we pursued the arts. A shared gallows humour and our longing for the ocean and surf and risk-taking adventure helped ease the confusion of our young-man blues. Because Frank had been a lifeguard and competitive swimmer, and I had always been a rabid waterman, we pool-hopped everywhere, climbing hedges and fences and plunging in. Frank was a superb high diver. At the Carleton pool he mesmerized everyone with his breathtaking swan dives. For effect, he'd stand erect until a crowd gathered. Then he'd spring up and arch out into space and down into the water with the classic style of an Acapulco diver in the movies.

Because I stopped drinking alcohol in the early seventies after driving into a telephone pole drunk-driving, and Frank never really drank, we had to find other ways of going off the deep end. At night, up in Quebec's Gatineau Hills, we enjoyed naked open-water swims in Pink Lake, which was fabled to be bottomless. Out in the middle of the lake, after belting out lines from Allen Ginsberg's *Howl* — "who howled on their knees in the subway and were dragged off the roof waving genitals and manuscripts" — we'd take in air and swim down in tandem. We descended until we were lost like turtles with rheumatism, and then we'd both gaze up and swim through darkness until we finally surfaced. Because it had been so damned scary, we'd begin laughing maniacally until we almost drowned and had to swim away from each other's madness to regain our composure. Frank and I shared an ability to "move wild laughter in the throat of death."

We were so surf-deprived, Frank brought his surfboard to my parents' cottage at Norway Bay, Quebec, and we took turns surfing behind my dad's boat, pulled by a tow rope through the water by a 50 h.p. Chrysler, wake-boarding decades before it was invented. Eventually, on long weekends, we went on surfaris to Cape Cod, surfing in the Atlantic swells, dancing together like madmen to keep our morgue-blue bodies warm after each session in the waves.

We'd make trips in Frank's rusted-out VW Karmann Ghia that had once been the backdrop for Frank's photo of himself in Dale's sleeveless black formal gown with his caption, "The end of the world in the usual dress in a night full of hope." Armed with a surfboard, wet suits, a tattered copy of Leonard Cohen's *Beautiful Losers*, a loaf of rye bread, a block of cheese and barely enough money to get down to surf the cape and back, Frank and I got it into our heads that we should drop in unannounced on Leonard Cohen. When we got to Cohen's Montreal house on St. Dominique and knocked on his little wooden door, a robed Buddhist monk answered and ushered us in. Cohen's mother had died and Lenny had just left to prepare for the funeral. Frank was in his element.

The origins of Frank's first feature film, *A Life*, began in the mid-seventies when we started wading around in Existentialism, Nihilism, Despair and the Void. We craved intensity. "I'm going crazy, you should document it," he once wrote. We spent a ghastly day in a local slaughterhouse, wading in blood, wandering among hanging corpses, smashed skulls, flayed cow hides and racks filled with hundreds of brains, hearts, tripe and livers. I accompanied Frank on regular visits to his grandmother and grandfather in their nursing home. Every Thursday night Frank came over to the apartment Dale and I rented, and we had long, strange, beautiful, hilarious, profound and often pretentious conversations late into the night about DEATH, ART and LIFE. We dreamed of a future when Dale would be a painter, I'd be a writer and Frank a filmmaker. Frank dated Dale's friends: Scotty, Margie and the two lovely Dianes. Dale wrangled a nude-modelling job for Frank because she was studying visual arts at the University of Ottawa. Frank proved to be a natural exhibitionist, until he got assigned to Dale's class, and then not surprisingly he became a little self-conscious. At parties Dale teased Frank by displaying her nude charcoal sketches of him. But what finished Frank's nude-modelling career happened at a high school gig while he dressed behind a curtain, and a big man came up from behind and asked in a deep voice, "Can I help you on with your clothes?"

We fed each other's rabid hunger for literature and cinema. Frank loved mad visionaries and fringe people who went against the grain to prove their detractors wrong. We'd sit for hours talking about the books on his shelves, filling up our ambitions and imaginations. We loved the moody darkness of Leonard Cohen's *The Favourite Game*, *The Spice-Box of Earth* and *Death of a Lady's Man*. For years Frank took to calling himself F after one of the characters in *Beautiful Losers*. I pointed out the structural wonders and intensity of Michael Ondaatje's innovative novel *Coming Through Slaughter* and my favourite, *The Collected Works of Billy the Kid*. The Beats excited us with their relentless search for It. Kerouac's characters Sal Paradise and Dean Moriarty, modelled after his roller-coaster friendship with Neil Cassady, became a kind of blueprint for our manic travel and zest for life.

There was an affinity with the painter Alex Colville, especially since Colville had attended Mount Allison University, where Frank's mom and Timothy Findley's partner Bill Whitehead met and developed a lifelong friendship. In some ways, Colville's life and art reminded me of Frank and his family. We were obsessed with Colville's "Pacific," which depicts a shirtless man leaning meditatively in an open glass doorway, contemplating the horizon of sky, ocean and a breaking wave. In the foreground is a table marked off with the numbers of a yardstick. On the edge of the table, a loaded revolver. Frank and I were drawn to the existential ambiguity this image evokes, and its whiff of suicide, and of course, being surfers, we loved the Californian wave. But the reality of "Pacific" is that it was painted in the fall of 1967 when Colville was teaching in Santa Cruz. The man was Colville; the gun, a 1935 Browning Colville had when he was a WWII artist; and the table with the yardstick, his old mother's sewing table. The brooding man was contemplating the waves and political instability of America in the wake of the first Kennedy assassination. So even though we had it dead wrong, the romantic image of mortality, measured with respect to time and an open landscape of the Pacific, stuck.

The other Colville image we gravitated toward was a serigraph, "High Diver." Two young men perch on the steel-girdered arch of a bridge spanning a river. A bicycle is parked in the foreground. One friend squats on the apex of the arch, waiting his turn, and watches while the other freefalls down to the river below. For Frank it captured a glorious, terrifying moment, the triumph of letting go in the face of fear, which he went on to explore again and again in his desert quests. On January 2, 1979, Frank sent me a letter with this fierce quote from Colville: "Art is one of the principal means by which a human being tries to compensate for, or complement, the restlessness of death and temporality."

I lent him my copy of Yukio Mishima's *Death in Midsummer and Other Stories,* and he was riveted to the blood-dripping story "Patriotism," about a Japanese officer who ceremoniously disembowels himself just before his wife stabs herself to death. In a letter dated "Saturday Night, 1980," Frank wrote: "A letter is an unannounced visit, the postman the agent of rude surprises. One ought to reserve an hour a week for receiving letters and afterwards take a bath. — Nietzsche. Let's remember Mishima packed his anus with cotton wool so he wouldn't evacuate his bowels when he committed hari-kari. Please. Remember. Rick. Frank."

We discussed suicide, constantly. For a long time we were caught in a drift toward suicide, and it turned up in most of our work. Frank's interest in suicide began as an intellectual flirtation that accelerated and then abated as his extreme philosophy insulated him from the deeper questions of life and death. But I've often been tormented by thoughts about how close Frank got to impulses of suicide, especially on his last trip to the Sahara, when he crossed the desert toward an almost certain death. I gave him Toronto novelist Juan Butler's violent, disturbing *The Garbageman*, whose opening paragraph has this arresting line: "I just lay there in perfect peace and contentment. Like a sultan. Or a corpse." For a time Frank was enamoured by *The Garbageman*'s sexual depravity and anarchy, and he may have taken English writer Colin Wilson's comment as a personal credo and challenge: "It is a kind of extreme, a boundary … The question is whether you now have the qualities to go beyond it." A decade later Butler committed suicide.

One of my favourite Frank residences, aside from his top-floor student digs on Somerset East or the lonely high-rise in Hull, was his apartment in an old building at 305 Gloucester Street. From the big window where he had his writing desk and office (Frank was the first person I knew who actually lived in his office), you could see a wonderful old maple tree that still stands today beside the towering high-rise that has replaced his building. Frank's charming, funny, intelligent girlfriend Annie, who was taller than him, and loved him wholeheartedly, used to sunbathe topless up on the roof, reading texts for her classics degree. Frank would often call and say, "Rick, I'm having a serious bout of meaninglessness. Why don't you fire over?" I'd be at Frank's all the time talking about how to drum up arts-grant money or our receding hairlines, drinking the chia seed milkshakes Frank concocted to help bring our hair back. I took him to get his first weight set and bench so he could pump iron in the apartment to bulk up for his Sahara trip. In the apartment we bantered about death, aging, art, self-promotional gimmicks, buoying each other up with dark humour and brilliant witticisms. Frank used to say, "Rick, we have to start getting some of this material down on paper. It's dynamite."

After a couple of years, the old building was condemned. But out of stubborn civil disobedience, and to save money, Frank squatted there for months, staying long after the power and water were turned off. One day he phoned to say I had to come over to see something incredible. After the building had been condemned and a family of Vietnamese boat people vacated the apartment across the hall, an old man came in off the street at the same time every day to shit in their empty apartment. Frank was always a student of the human condition, fascinated by anything extreme. When we opened the door, the stench of human excrement nearly killed us on the spot. The walls were punched and battered, and defaced with crude, abstract expressionist graffiti. But what was worse, the entire apartment was ankle-deep in dead cockroaches. They had gone mad and multiplied after the Vietnamese family left. For whatever twisted reason, the old man kept breaking into the abandoned apartment, walking across the dead cockroaches, then squatting down to have a shit in various spots in the apartment. When Frank led me to a bathtub filled with dead cockroaches, all I could say was, "Reminds me of the scene in the barn filled with rats from Ondaatje's *Billy the Kid*." A couple of weeks later, after repeated unanswered phone calls, and because Frank and I were always half-afraid one of us would do himself in, I went to his apartment. When I couldn't find him, I panicked. I searched every empty room in the spooky building. Finally I went up through a passageway to the roof and found Frank sitting crossed-legged in the sun. He was drinking one of his small cups of black Turkish coffee as if he were on an Algerian rooftop chatting about the myth of Sisyphus with Albert Camus.

Frank was a minimalist. He retained only what was essential for his every-day life. At his 305 Gloucester Street apartment, and later in his Riverside Drive apartment, his spartan bookshelves contained several editions of his favourite book, Antoine de Saint-Exupéry's classic children's story for adults, *The Little Prince*. Frank modelled his character/persona Howard Stone for his first feature film, *A Life*, from *The Little Prince* — right down to the tight grey uniform and diminutive figure overwhelmed by an empty desert. Frank also read and reread *Wind, Sand and Stars*, Saint-Exupéry's memoir about desert flight, duty, honour and courage. Like Frank, Saint-Exupéry left for a trip and never returned. There were copies of Timothy Findley's *The Wars*, *The Butterfly Plague*, *Last of the Crazy People* and *Famous Last Words*. Because Tiff was such a literary icon, Frank and I looked up to him as a kind of mentor. But Tiff, like all established writers assailed by unpublished writers, was lukewarm about our creative projects. On the Ottawa leg of their book tours, Bill Whitehead and Tiff stayed with the Coles, and I'd be invited by Frank to formal dinner parties. Once, to the horror of eight politely pissed-off guests at the dinner table, I pulled out an unpublished manuscript of my short story "Broken Harmony" and proceeded to read it. Later on Tiff forgave us both, and as Frank's films were produced and I began publishing, he wrote congratulatory letters.

Frank's bookshelves contained well-thumbed copies of Norman O. Brown's *Love's Body*, and more importantly *Life Against Death: The Psychoanalytic Meaning of History*. Frank was always talking to me about Brown, an influential

California university professor and mind-expanding writer from the sixties. Like Frank, Brown was obsessed with death, and had a mind full of demons he channelled into his art, yet he, too, was a gentle-souled, sweet man. Frank internalized Brown's psychology and philosophy, synthesizing these into his own life and work. Brown said individuals and society were imprisoned by an essentially Freudian ill: repression. He argued that the only escape was to face death head-on and affirm life.

Frank's library also included Hubert Selby Jr.'s *Last Exit to Brooklyn*, which is about homosexuals and transvestites. Jean Genet's *Our Lady of the Flowers* led to Céline's *Death on the Installment Plan* and John Rechy's novels of homosexuality and male hustling — *City of Night*, *Rushes* and *The Sexual Outlaw: A Documentary*. Frank flirted with an ambiguous sexuality and he often referred to himself in a deep voice as "the Sexual Outlaw." For a couple of years, before his "celibate" stage, Frank would obsessively go to Hull, dancing alone into the small hours in throbbing gay bars like Le Club. To feed his slightly fascist tendencies of rigorous discipline, precision and planning, and because he admired self-scrutiny, Frank read Albert Speer's *Spandau: The Secret Diaries*. Speer had been Hitler's architect for the Third Reich and, by pleading guilty, he managed to escape the death penalty many of his Nazi cohorts had received. Instead, Speer endured twenty years in solitary confinement, where he painstakingly wrote his life story on rolls of toilet paper that were smuggled out. After he was released from prison, he eventually wrote and published two volumes about his life in the Third Reich. To survive long Ottawa winters, one of the things Frank and I discussed was Speer's survival tactic, whereby he imagined himself travelling to various places in the world, without leaving the confines of his jail cell.

Aside from the Koran, which Frank read and reread, he also possessed several desert classics. The first was Geoffrey Moorhouse's *The Fearful Void*, a travel memoir about the author's brave but failed attempt to cross the Sahara alone. Frank corresponded with him for a couple of years, and Moorhouse wrote back with helpful information Frank later used for his first desert crossing. In 1992, while I was living for a year in Hong Kong, I met Moorhouse, who was promoting a new book, *Hell's Foundations: A Town, Its Myths, and Gallipoli.* Moorhouse talked to me about Frank's obsession with going back to the desert yet again: "You can tell Frank that crossing the Sahara is a young man's game." Years later in an interview, Moorhouse said something ironic when applied to Frank: "Whatever it is that you are frightened of the most, is never quite as bad when you actually encounter it."

Another writer Frank corresponded with was Michael Asher, who wrote *Impossible Journey: Two Against the Sahara*, which chronicles the author's journey with his wife, Mariantonietta. They travelled 4,500 miles in a westward crossing of the Sahara in 1986–87. Asher's book helped to spur Frank on in his own epic journey. But the man and the book that really fuelled Frank's desires and aspirations were T. E. Lawrence and *Seven Pillars of Wisdom*. The book was always there, and Frank even gave me an inscribed copy before I left for French Polynesia to research a book I was writing about the final years of Paul Gauguin in the South Seas: "Rick, take only this to the hotel. F. 24.12.82." At one point *A Life* was subtitled *A Campaign*, which might help explain Frank's admiration for Lawrence's self-discipline, courage, vision and military genius. He also respected the way Lawrence in later life returned to being an ordinary bloke. Lawrence lived a celibate, intellectual life with books and carried on the physical love of riding his motorcycle in the isolated hill country in the southwest of England. Many times, on the big screen of the Mayfair Theatre, Frank and I crossed the Sinai desert with Peter O'Toole in David Lean's masterpiece, *Lawrence of Arabia*. The gruelling desert crossings and Lawrence's mystical death as he gloriously roared along the narrow hedgerows until his motorcycle crashed seemed unbearably romantic — a poetic ending to a short, heroic life that stirred Frank no end. Frank was very heavily inspired and influenced by many films we saw together, including *The Night Porter*, *Last Tango in Paris*, *The Conformist*, *Walkabout*, *The Conversation*, *The American Friend*, *Lightning Over Water*, *Fitzcarraldo*, *Burden of Dreams*, *The Tenant*, *Taxi Driver*, *Apocalypse Now* and *Death in Venice*.

A spooky midnight showing of David Lynch's *Eraserhead* deadened me to the core, and when we staggered out of the theatre and I confessed how depressing I thought the film was, Frank began laughing until I thought his head would fall off his shoulders. Depressing films seemed to buoy him up with hope. Hal Ashby's black comedy about suicide, *Harold and Maude*, was a grim treat, especially since it starred Ruth Gordon, who had been one of Timothy Findley's close friends.

Maverick Canadian film director Budge Crawley became an idol for Frank. When we filmed *A Life*, we met old Crawley, and his Ottawa-based Crawley Films even let Frank use its equipment and a veteran lighting specialist named Lucky. Crawley's Academy Award–winning documentary *The Man Who Skied Down Everest* showed Frank how the obsession of one man to conquer a landscape can be validated by art, though eight people died so the Japanese skier could realize his dream, and another man, Budge Crawley, could make his documentary film.

As I wrote stories and sent them off, only to be rejected by editors, Frank tried to get into the prestigious film school in Paris to follow Jean-Luc Godard and the New Wave French cinema. But he ended up at the now-defunct film program at Algonquin College in Ottawa, where he mentored under the charismatic film professor Peter Evanchuck. Frank was the only one of his graduating class to finish his own film. In an article he said, "I owe an awful lot to Peter Evanchuck. He taught me a lot and I attribute much of my motivation and success to him." While pursuing his role as an *enfant terrible*, Frank produced *A Documentary* in 1979, an unsparing work chronicling the cancer death of his grandmother. Many were shocked, but it impressed at festivals around the world. Frank's grandmother's death left his grandfather so bereft and alone that Frank decided in his art and his life to challenge the archetypal experience of death itself.

Just after *A Documentary* was finished, Frank and I got together with Peter Azmier, Dushin Mirkovich and Peter Evanchuck to write a scary little 116-page black book called *Last Resort*. We each had fifteen to twenty pages. On the back cover, below a group photo that looked like an outlaw rock band, was the book blurb: "This introduces a new group of writers — with varied styles but with a conscious, unified clarity of life on the edge. They move across historic pulses, each instant a lived time. With anger, despair and hope they move into the eighties." The book was loosely modelled in style, content and themes after the Beat writers: Kerouac, Ginsberg, Cassady and Burroughs. *Last Resort* was a subversive anthology of disturbing autobiographical material, with Evanchuck as the driving force. He was an extremely influential early supporter of Frank's work in film and helped Frank come out of his meek shell, though Peter's impatient, angry personality ultimately went against Frank's gentle, methodical nature.

But *Last Resort* was an underground hit. Our book launch at Paul King's Food for Thought bookstore in the Market opened on the street with a saxophone player and a stripper. We did a wild performance at Saw Gallery, where I dressed in a big fur coat and punched my hand through a suspended glass window. At Splash Gallery, Peter had a solo installation, *Rainbow Exhibits*, whose entranceway consisted of a gnarly, undulating walk-through vulva. His section of the book dealt with strippers from Arnprior to Key West, suicide, drugs, despair and Mayan pyramids. Frank's section, "The Death," was a warm-up act for *A Life*, and began: "I was born in 1954. Twenty-six years are over. I know what time it is. I have judged myself, and I find myself immoral. Somehow I must hope, there is a place, of order." His pages were saturated with

death, suicide as crucifixion, coitus as neurosis, mortality, miracles, mothers, transvestites, celibacy. His bio at the end of the book simply stated: "Frank Cole is in the North Africa desert; and if returning will direct a feature film, about death."

My autobiographical prose poems were eventually integrated into several other books over the years. One of my pieces, "The Road," celebrated Frank's Gloucester Street apartment, with a framed Van Gogh reproduction that was the only painting on Frank's walls and was purported to be the artist's last painting. Frank photographed several severe self-portraits inspired by Van Gogh's despair. For my first book, *Tender Only to One*, I had been researching and writing about Vincent van Gogh and Paul Gauguin's short, demonic cohabitation in the famous Yellow House in Arles, where van Gogh cut off his ear, then committed suicide. Frank saw me as a Gauguin figure, and himself as van Gogh. Both in our letters and on the phone we called each other Paul and Vincey. "The Road" revealed where we were at the time, and in light of Frank's desert demise, its disappearing road proved prophetic.

The process of writing, editing, publishing and promoting *Last Resort* was a bizarre roller-coaster ride that proved beneficial to Frank and myself. In the end we learned how to hype ourselves. It helped us obtain grants, and gain credibility and confidence so we could both move forward with our artistic projects. To obtain film funding, Frank became a wizard at self-promotion. He had remarkable drive and self-discipline, and an endearing way of acquiring money from the various arts councils.

For years, Frank nurtured a sexual ambiguity he loved to flaunt. He had a weird aura of menace and penetrating eye contact. But when you really got to know Frank, he was a puppy dog who possessed great warmth and generosity. He was always offering to help people. Over the years he attracted a long line of fine women who were drawn to his thoughtful, impeccable politeness and disarming presence. Like everyone who knew Frank, women either embraced his intense dark side or avoided it. All of his girlfriends appreciated Frank's unique intensity, and all of them had first names ending in vowels: Jacey, Melissa, Annie, Janey, Venetia, Pucchi and Sonia.

In the early eighties, Frank talked me into being assistant director for his first feature film, initially called *A Death*. Later, I went over to see him at the apartment because he'd worked out a new title. I waited through one of Frank's famously pregnant pauses before he announced, triumphantly, "*A Life.*" I burst out laughing and then he followed. We laughed and coughed and laughed and then we wiped the tears from our eyes. At one time it was going to be called *The Meaning of History*. In any event, it was Frank's original reinterpretation of certain themes from Norman O. Brown's *Life Against Death: The Psychoanalytical Meaning of History*, and a little of John Rechy's *The Sexual Outlaw: A Documentary* (minus the hardcore sex) and *The Little Prince*, T. E. Lawrence and all the other books and films Frank had assimilated over the years, along with his own mixed stew of personal demons, all fuel-injected by his relentless drive.

A Life charts a man's survival amid death in a room and in the desert. Ottawa artist Lea Deschamps kindly gave up her rambling second-storey artist's studio on Sparks Street for the shoot, which began at the end of a summer heat wave. We removed Lea's belongings so we could start with an empty room. We reskinned and refurnished it to create Frank's austere nightmare of minimalism. Frank demanded perfection, and every detail took an eternity. The film set was as pared down as the stage set for Samuel Beckett's *Waiting for Godot*, or a Harold Pinter play. Piece by piece we laid out a new wooden floor, constructed walls from huge frames of wood stapled with canvas that was painted white. In one corner we put in a bathtub with a linoleum floor. We built a window whose bottom edge was a sharp guillotine blade. Our talented art director, Elie Abdel-Ahad, painted a haunting blue-sky backdrop. When the sky was backlit, it cast mesmerizing geometric blocks of sunlight through the window onto the wooden floor and white walls of the empty room. Looking across to that sunlit window of open sky, which flooded the room with light, was like being in a disembodied chamber of heaven. For years we'd talked about van Gogh's painting of his empty bedroom with the bed, chair, bedside table and wooden floor. What Frank had recreated in the set for *A Life* was the loneliness of van Gogh's desire to make art out of the bare furnishings of a simple bedroom. He had stumbled upon the perfect setting for Blaise Pascal's much-quoted dictum about man's inability to sit quietly in a shuttered room.

We loaded cars with a bed, dressers, end tables, a bookcase, a telephone and other props from his parents' house in Alta Vista. Frank's patient father, Charles, helped me move furnishings into the studio. I can still remember the sidelong glance of bewilderment Charles flashed while we humped his family furniture up the studio stairs in murderous heat. I'm sure he was trying to get his head around this challenging phase of his son's life as an uncompromising independent filmmaker.

Like most film directors, Frank was under tremendous pressure. And like most directors, Frank was a control freak's control freak. He had written the film, drummed up funding and now he was overseeing the construction of a set that had to compete with the vast emptiness of the Sahara. Frank was also directing, acting and trying to hold the whole mess together through a sheer act of will. All of this before he had to leave for the gruelling desert shoot. With so many peopled demands, I joked with Frank about how I have total control of my book, whereas for a filmmaker, the artistic process is like trying to run an airline.

Frank had received some grant money, and at first he thought he had to feed the crew. A few times he took us to restaurants, but it started getting out of hand, until we told everyone to eat before they came, or bring lunches. Of course, everything to do with the film took much longer than planned. We had to constantly improvise, beg, borrow and occasionally steal things to construct the set and shoot the film.

The Peruvian cameraman from Montreal, Carlos Ferrand, had directed his own films and was already a consummate professional. Everyone respected Carlos and listened to him when he suggested ways to get on with Frank's meticulous shooting schedule, from Monday, August 22, to Sunday, September 4. Frank's schedule contained brief descriptions such as: *Removal of furnishings. Wake up and stand at window. Room as desert. H. Stone monologue. Esperanza Stone attempted suicide. Stone vs. snake. Attempted suicide: snake bite, and snake decapitation. E. Stone (child) age four attempted suicide. Night. Stranger on highway.*

We had a weight bench on the edge of the studio, so Frank and I could pump iron. Wearing a red bandana headband, tight shorts and no shirt, I looked equal parts Geronimo and Tarzan. Frank was at the peak of his weightlifting prime. Like little Hulk, he padded barefoot around the set in his skimpy shorts, dripping with perspiration because of the humidity and no air conditioner. Late one afternoon, while Frank stood spotting me as I lay on the bench about to perform a heavy bench press, the woman originally slated to play Esperanza Stone arrived out of nowhere. She stood face to face with Frank, who had come in front of me to meet her. He looked a little worried. Lying on the bench, I stared up helplessly. Suddenly she reached under her skirt and pulled out a long rubber snake. Then she proceeded to viciously lash Frank back and forth across his face and bare upper body. Frank just stood there taking the beating. When she stopped, he was wide-eyed, in shock. But stoic. Deep welts

stood out on his face, chest and shoulders. She tossed the snake at him, turned on her high heels and strutted out of the room. Frank and I were speechless. In the back pages of magazines, weightlifter Charles Atlas had promised skinny guys that by lifting iron, big men on beaches would no longer kick sand in their faces. But Charles Atlas never said anything about how to cope with disgruntled women. That evening, in exasperation, Frank said, "All I want to do is make my little film."

Some evenings, instead of going home to his parents' place where he was living to save money, Frank slept on the hard wooden floor in the empty room to clear his head. He had been denying himself creature comforts to help get in the mood for his role in the film, and to get ready for those long uncomfortable nights sleeping in the desert. For a few months in someone's O'Connor Street basement, he even slept with his girlfriend in a tent, crammed in between a washer and dryer and furnace, in order to help prepare for the Sahara.

Everyone worked on *A Life* for nothing; some believed the project might find its way into Canadian film history. There were many friends and talented people involved: an art director, cameramen, lighting people and a few actors. There were also grasshoppers and crickets to feed the mice that were fed to the snakes that were kept in boxes and scared the shit out of everyone. With the humidity and all those people, insects, rodents and reptiles, it smelled like the back alley of a North African village.

Several people jump-started their careers by working on Frank's film. I put in a whole summer helping to shoot the studio sequences, shot by painstaking shot. It took days to set up the decisive moment when a little girl had to run through a sliding glass window. Constructing the tall window was like preparing a gallows. The little girl and her parents and the crew all hung back, waiting nervously as the tall window was fitted with fake glass. The little girl, who was playing Esperanza Stone, sat meekly on the edge of the bed in a little grey uniform that matched the uniform of her adult counterpart. She was the embodiment of the Little Prince. Another window was rigged with the long sharp blade of a guillotine ready to drop. Everyone was fascinated, unnerved, yet strangely proud of our guillotine. The grown-up version of Esperanza was played by Anne Miquet. Her talented brother Francis would go on to produce *Life Without Death* and support Frank for all the years it took to bring that film to the screen. Some days there was a palpable sexual tension on the set, especially during the nude scenes, with blood in Esperanza's bathtub and a gun in her panties. There were scenes where a large snake moved across the whole length of the floor and scared everyone off the set, except Frank. I had to herd everyone back into the room to face the snake while it skittered, whipping and slashing around. People hid behind furniture, up on the bed, and several climbed the stepladder. The crickets we fed the mice that were in turn fed to the snakes got loose. From time to time we heard the eerie sound of crickets between the walls of the set and Lea's apartment. As assistant director, my job was to choreograph this surreal Noah's Ark of artificial despair.

Frank asked me to accompany him to the Sahara to shoot the second half of the film. We would drive 17,000 kilometres, looking for site locations. But I declined. I had my own writing projects to get on with, and I knew Frank would not be stopping to smell the roses along the way. He would treat it like a mission from hell, and we'd be as far away from water as you can get here on earth. I didn't tell Frank that I was afraid to go with him and I thought I might never return alive. Every trip to the Sahara meant another brush with death and sooner or later something bad would happen. But I did sign a waiver on February 27, 1984, that read: "This is to certify that in the event of my death, Richard Taylor as Assistant Director of my film, *A Death*, has my authorization to complete it. The workprint is stored at 1478 Orchard Ave. The Original Negative is stored at Medallion Laboratory, Toronto. Frank Cole."

A Life premiered in 1986. The Canadian Film Institute described its taut visual style as a "searing psychological and physical excursion into cycles of death, life and redemption … a remarkable accomplishment." Film critic Geoff Pevere wrote, "*A Life* is quite unlike anything made in this country before." The late Jay Scott described Frank as reclusive, enigmatic and brilliant.

Of course, with reviews such as those, Frank decided to hit the road again and cross the Sahara to make an even more ambitious film he wanted to call *Death's Death*. Years later, his producer, Francis Miquet, convinced him to retitle it *Life Without Death*. Unfortunately, the film took ten years to reach the big screen. To prepare himself for the ordeal of making the film, Frank pumped up by lifting weights. He attended extensive first-aid courses, learned about camels, survival, celestial navigation and astronomy, and he reread the Koran and T. E. Lawrence's *Seven Pillars of Wisdom*.

I'd been pestering Frank to keep a journal of his desert crossing and wrote a letter of recommendation for an arts grant so he could write a book on the trip. Frank really didn't want to write, but I badgered him over and over again, knowing it would be an important document. I joked with Frank, "Writing the book will be harder than crossing the desert." Early in the trip I got a postcard from the Saharan city Nouakchott:

November 19, 1989
Dear Rick, I got myself on that flight from Morocco to Mauritania, but my bags didn't. They were lost. But I got them back twelve days later. For the last five of those days, when I'd finished everything I had to do, it was because of your insistence that I write my book, that I still had a life. This'll happen again many times ahead. Frank.

To shoot his film, Frank had to do virtually the impossible — cross the Sahara alone. He went through eight camels, was arrested, got lost, travelled through war zones, was stalked by murderous thieves, attacked by one of his own camels and, for eleven months, had to deal with exhaustion, fear and loneliness. Each night he slept out in the open under the stars, listening to the wind.

Not only did Frank cross the desert, he had to film the whole journey himself. Because I had supervised the film crew's time-consuming shoots in the relatively pristine conditions of the Sparks Street studio, I can imagine what photographing himself crossing the desert must have entailed. I know how scary, uncomfortable, even masochistic, it must have been. And it would take its toll.

When he returned from the desert, Frank became a recluse, and worked to complete *Life Without Death*. It was his Sistine Chapel, his mistress and his albatross. He had to drum up more funds and do most of the work himself.

He began a merciless Life Extension diet and pushed literature for the Life Extension Foundation. He signed up with the Cryonics Institute. In between long bouts of film work, he got back into surfing in Baja, California, Peru and Puerto Escondido. Often he camped on open beaches, living on a diet of carrots, lettuce, pasta and rice. He would send me photos of himself surfing vertical walls of three-metre bone crushers. At Camp Fortune, where he met his future girlfriend Sonia, he became a dedicated ski patroller. They did a couple of surf trips together as well as a harrowing canoe trip through the Florida Everglades to discover the source of the world's hungriest mosquitoes. Yet unbelievably, during this time, he was planning another trip to Africa to cross the Sahara.

Meanwhile, for me, between teaching, writing, a strangling mortgage, a wife and two growing daughters, Sky and Quinn — all of the things Frank had managed to avoid — my life had never been busier. We spoke on the phone occasionally, and I should have spent more time with him, but like all long-term friendships, our relationship had its dry spells and reconciliations. Over the years I had to pull away from Frank. His films and obsessions lasted decades, including his identification with death itself. I had small daughters who I had decided to look after as a Mr. Mom while Dale worked, so for a decade my time and energy were almost completely gobbled up. Frank was so single-minded and unencumbered, he sometimes lost sight of other people's responsibilities outside of their creative work. I had to live out my own demons my own way. Our obsessions with mortality were at once similar and distinct, and we needed space.

In late 1996, Frank was so happy for me that I was going back to Byron Bay, Australia, to live in a beach house where I could write and surf for a year. But a month before I left, my sister Jan and my four-year-old nephew died in a house fire in Chelsea, Quebec. Frank wrote to say how devastated he was about my sister's death. Death truly shook him to the core. A month later I finally got away from Ottawa to live in Australia with my family. I had unplugged from the rat race and began writing my travel memoir *House Inside the Waves: Domesticity, Art and the Surfing Life*. After I wrote Frank about surfing the reefs with sharks and on waves the size of drive-in movie screens, he sent one of his short, cryptic postcards, almost exactly three years before he was murdered: "October 17, 97. Ottawa. Rick, if you crank it up any more, you'll come back in a body bag. Vincey."

A few years later, in October 2000, just before Halloween, I received a wrenching phone call from Sonia, who had been living in Frank's Riverside Drive apartment while he was crossing the Sahara. Frank was dead. For several decades I had expected such a call. Once he even joked about getting a T-shirt made that said, "Frank Cole Is Dead." But even though his death came as no real surprise, the sudden loss of a long-time friend, and the manner of his brutal death, left me drained and shaken. Sonia said she had been receiving regular emails from Frank in Africa, via External Affairs. But the week before Halloween, Frank's body had been discovered by a shepherd. His two camels had been stolen, along with his camera equipment and clothes. He had been tied up and murdered 70 kilometres southeast of Timbuktu, near the Niger River in Mali.

Frank was constantly obsessed with the desert. For years he had been talking about returning to the Sahara. Everyone agreed it was a bad idea. I suggested that if he felt compelled to go back to Africa, he should surf the coastline, live it up a little and forget about crossing that hellish desert. I even shared a dream with Frank about surfing the coast of Africa with him. But the Sahara's siren call and his confusion about heroism finally caught up with him. For many years in our manic conversations about famous writers, filmmakers and artists, we had laughed about the ambiguous concept of heroism, and how some people have it despite logic, reason and common sense.

I went to see Frank the day before he left Canada for the desert. I wanted to give him a copy of the travel anthology *Literary Trips: Following in the Footsteps of Fame*. It contained my piece about Bruce Chatwin that later became the first chapter of *House Inside the Waves*. Chatwin was a famous travel writer, photographer and world traveller who tragically died of AIDS at age forty-eight. His notion about man's restlessness and inability to stay inside a room was something both Frank and I wrestled with for nearly thirty years. Frank would have read this on the verge of leaving for the Sahara. The essay begins, "Even before I left Canada for Australia, I had quickly jotted down some questions posed in the jacket copy of Bruce Chatwin's Australian odyssey, *The Songlines*, which I now pondered: 'Why is man the most restless, dissatisfied of animals? Why do wandering people conceive the world as perfect whereas sedentary ones always try to change it? Why have the great teachers — Christ or the Buddha — recommended the Road as the way to salvation?'" The ending of my piece clearly draws, in retrospect, parallels between Frank's life and death: "Wandering may have settled some of Chatwin's natural curiosity and urge to explore, but he was always tugged back by a longing for a real home he never found. He had a strong compulsion to roam and perhaps an equally strong need to return, a homing instinct like that of a migrating bird. An unfortunate irony, given Chatwin's death shortly after *The Songlines* was published, is illustrated on the last page of the book when he says that mystics believed the ideal man will walk himself to a 'right death' because he who has arrived 'goes back.'"

As a parting gift, Frank gave me two films, labelled in his own meticulous fashion with his name, address and film title. One was a documentary, *The Lure of Surfing*, a soulful, warm-hearted movie about the joys and mystique of surfing. Frank said I could keep it, adding that he didn't need it anymore. He also handed me a 1997 documentary by Werner Herzog called *Little Dieter Needs to Fly* that was his favourite. It opens with a quote from Revelations 9:6: "And in those days shall men seek death, and shall not find it, and shall desire to die, and death shall flee from them." Herzog takes Dieter Dengler back to Vietnam so the ex-POW can confront his worst fears again, which is something Frank was always doing — confronting fear and challenging death. Frank liked to emulate larger-than-life characters like Alexander the Great, Mishima and little Dieter Dengler, who says in the film, "I'm not a hero. Only dead people are heroes." Something obviously resonated between Herzog and Dengler that warmed Frank's own obsessive-compulsive heart, and perhaps helped to jump-start his creative spirit and impel a return to the Sahara.

Before I met up with Frank, my literary editor, Victoria Brooks, had gone to visit another man with an affinity for the desert — Paul Bowles. He was an American expat whose novel *The Sheltering Sky* had been made into a Bertolucci film I had seen on the big screen with Frank in the early nineties. (Years later Frank and his producer Francis managed to get the people who did the music for *The Sheltering Sky* to do music for *Life Without Death*.) Bowles had left America for more than forty years to live as a recluse in North Africa. A literary cult legend, he constantly wrote about westerners going to the Sahara only to be annihilated by their own shortcomings or murdered by thieves.

In a book of travel essays about the non-Christian world, Paul Bowles wrote a piece about the Sahara called "The Baptism of Solitude." I still have the ragged quote I ripped from the book and once shared with Frank: "When a man has been there and undergone the baptism of solitude, he can't help himself. Once he has been under the spell of the vast, luminous silent country, no other place is quite strong enough for him, no other surroundings can provide the supremely satisfying sensation of existing in the midst of something that is absolute. He will go back, whatever the cost in comfort and money, for the absolute has no price."

During the summer I got my last letter from Frank: "June 29, 2000. Nouakchott, Mauritania. Rick, Thanks both for your book and your visit. I left Cap Blanc, Mauritania on April 21. Now, after two months and 1000 km., I've been forced back to the beginning again — The Atlantic. Frank."

On November 4, about a week after the news of Frank's death, *Life Without Death* opened at the Canadian Film Institute. It was described as "a disturbing meditation on mortality's ever ticking clock," and all the sad ironies were too clear. Only a handful of us at the opening, including Sonia, myself and Dale, knew that Frank was dead. The rest of the audience was told some romantic bullshit about Frank riding a camel somewhere in the Sahara near Timbuktu.

Over the next few weeks, whenever I was out at night walking our collie Ruby in the deserted park, I'd be haunted by Frank's murder. I'd look back over my shoulder as I walked in the dark, and then hurry home with the dog. Over and over I imagined his last moments. My youngest daughter, Quinn, spent the next few weeks sleeping on the floor beside her sister's bed because she didn't want to be alone in her room. Dale and I had to read long into many nights to fall asleep. Finally, it was only by writing about him that I slowly began to cope with his death.

I spoke with Frank's parents, Charles and Jean, and his brother Peter. Because of my sister's death a few years earlier, I could empathize with the Coles' nightmare. Finally, after more than a month of red tape, Frank's body was flown from Bamako, the capital of Mali, to Brussels and then to the Cryonics Institute in Detroit. Dental records and a DNA sample confirmed that the small skeleton was, in fact, the earthly remains of Frank Cole.

There are still many wild theories about Frank's murder. Probably no one will ever find out who killed Frank, or why. Just as no one will ever really know why Frank had to go back and cross the desert again. Timbuktu is one of those places whose name is linked to the romance of desert exploration. But for more than thirty years travellers have been warned about the dangers of journeying across Mali. In a country with so much political unrest, poverty and hunger, a privileged westerner travelling alone on a camel must be a kind of sacrilegious mirage, and a great temptation for revenge.

In his heart, I'm sure Frank realized the desert was not the best place to endure solitude. Like many, though, he still hadn't found what he was looking for. Perhaps he wanted to take one last trip before beginning a new life with people. Frank once said, "My art is a blueprint for my life. I work best against bad odds." He wanted immortality, not celebrity. He wasn't willing to accept the inevitability of death. On an earlier trip across the Sahara, Frank thought he saw the devil. This time, he met him.

I introduced my friend, landscape painter Joan Sutherland, to Frank more than ten years ago. She received one of Frank's last letters on October 11, a week before he was murdered: "Joanie — Even in Timbuktu, you are not forgotten. I took 6 months and 3,000 km riding to get across the first country, Mauritania. Five countries still to go. Sahara feels endless. I long for life to be so endless too. Frank."

Frank and I had got a long way from that first meeting in our Carleton University Spanish class in 1972. We had travelled the world, surfed, swam and had women love us despite our dreams. From our Thursday-night discussions in the early seventies with Dale, where we confessed our hopes for the future, and after our van was stolen in the Donald Duck parking lot in Florida and I lost my early manuscripts, Dale's early paintings and Frank's first film, I went on to write better books, Dale painted better paintings and Frank made better films. Frank's saltwater road began in the surf of Cape Town, South Africa, and ended in North Africa, in landlocked Mali near the terminus of the Salt Road of Timbuktu, where slaves, gold, ivory and blocks of salt from the dried-up lakes in the desert were transported by camels across the Sahara.

In June 1978, while Dale and I were preparing for a trip to surf around the world, and Frank was preparing for his own trip, he wrote:

Dear Rick and Daley,

You've been on the road a few hours now, and I felt it was the time to write. You know there wasn't really anything left to discuss Thursday night — it had really all been discussed over the past several months. I needn't have been frantic. There are just a few things I want to say: Many thanks for all the help and encouragement you gave me this year. I needed it. I'm looking very forward to the next year and a half and all its agony and ecstasy and its revelations and in seeing you again in the end. In the true contradictory style of life I am also not looking forward to that … in that it puts us that much further down the road. You are right when you say Rick, that "every" year is an important year. There are no unimportant years. I just hope we all make it back to tell the story. Ha! I know I haven't yet felt the impact of your going. I wanted to say that I think we should keep these letters. I mean this. We may want them in the future. There is a story here and other things. I'll have you know that I refused an invitation to stay the night at the girl's place, after we left you. I tell you this just to confuse you further. Until later. Love Frank.

"There is always another way to tell the story." — *Norman O. Brown*

I thought you'd beat the inevitability of death
to death
just a little bit
    — The Tragically Hip

The phone rings. I pick up the receiver. A monotone voice says my name. "Tom."
I say yes. There is a long pause.
"It's Frank Cole."

He is in his barren apartment on Riverside Drive in Ottawa. There is the hint of an echo from the room in which he is calling. We discuss the film-funding proposals we had read separately as jurors for the Independent Filmmakers Co-operative of Ottawa.

To say we speak is misleading. Conversations with Frank Cole are less speaking than they are disquieting excursions into aural arrhythmia and silence. Frank's deliberate, glacially paced remarks cleave enormous slabs of silence out of utterances. Talking to him, I find myself slowing down, measuring my words with care. Slowly, more slowly, even more slowly. There is more silence than sound on the phone. I discover that this initially unsettling navigation of Frank's intermittent monotone articulation is pleasurable, even relaxing; a conversation with Frank Cole has a palpable way of taking its time. Taking all of time itself. It is a gradual immersion in a place where time can be heard again. I can feel it hovering on the line in the slight trembling of the telephone cord. It is strange and refreshing. After many protracted pauses and words patiently waited for and eventually uttered, we arrive at which films will receive co-op funding.

Before he hangs up, he laughs. A genuine, husky, eager, almost giddy laugh. It is a laugh that says we did it, it is a sound of relief. And now — the laugh intimates as it fades — it's on to the next zone of dread.

Frank was a man at war. On the half-dozen occasions when we met, he possessed the air of a veteran of an obscure, mysteriously violent campaign. Or so I imagined. His charismatic, subtly intimidating presence made me imagine that he had seen rare and sinister and wondrous things. He seemed to have access to something I did not and could not even imagine.

On the other hand, he was typically Canadian in his confrontations with vast, hostile and emptied landscapes. He was some other Terry Fox on some other marathon. Crossing and recrossing a continent of sand, he wrote a life's story in a book of sand, adhering to a tenacious, disciplined monotony. Stride after stride, he wrested form out of the hot, sandy temporal trudge. Walking was his war, and it was always fought in no-man's land, alone under black-hole darkness or searing incandescence.

Another whispering night is upon me. I know how to sleep on this bed of dry oceanic terrain. Will I die out here? I've been warned of the lawlessness and desperation. But I've done this before. There are always warnings. I have seen no one around me. I will bed down under this tree. I will be awakened by the desert's gathering inferno and the stubborn scratching of trees and bushes against the arid air. I will wake up.

Fyodor Dostoevsky once observed that his Russian capital, St. Petersburg, was a "premeditated city," where the social atmosphere is dominated by silent strategies of identity control, careful attention to one's social behaviour and a paranoiac concern with regulating individual passion. In many ways, Ottawa is similar: it possesses a cautious personality with a quiet obsession with discretion. Beneath this surface, however, as in Dostoevsky's Russia, outrage and irrationality look for an outlet. The dark fissures in this ordered city can be seen in the sensibility of Frank Cole, a man whose intense expression arises out of a culture of control, not only as an inhabitant of Ottawa, but also as the son of a diplomat whose cultural currency is necessarily restraint and moderation.

In 1939, the National Film Board of Canada was established in Ottawa, a government institution that spawned not only Canada's storied documentary tradition, but also, in the gifted hands of a young animator named Norman McLaren, the nation's equally fabled avant-garde, experimental film tradition. In Ottawa? Conservative, repressed, careful, "premeditated" Ottawa? City of bureaucrats, blazers, briefcases, minor conspiracies and hidden agendas? Yes, Ottawa.

Unlikely as it seems today, Ottawa was, at least until the NFB moved its head office and production facilities to Montreal in 1956, the epicentre of filmmaking in Canada. Outside the NFB, Ottawa's independent film company, Crawley Films, produced dozens of sponsored films and documentaries, and in the 1960s began to make feature films, including *The Luck of Ginger Coffey* and *Amanita Pestilens*. In 1975 it won the Academy Award for best documentary with *The Man Who Skied Down Everest*. Few independent filmmakers worked in the area, however, as most filmmaking talent left for the emerging production centres of Montreal, Toronto or Vancouver. Lacking a critical mass of practitioners and fighting the perception that a government town is a creative wasteland, after the NFB left, the remaining Ottawa filmmakers went underground.

In the mid-1970s, at Algonquin College, Frank Cole learned the craft of film-making under the tutelage of Peter Evanchuck. At the same time, Carleton University was creating a film studies department with such luminaries as Peter Harcourt encouraging the study and appreciation of Canadian cinema. The city developed a lively critical and film exhibition community, with the Canadian Film Institute's cinematheque as well as an excellent repertory cinema (the Towne and, later, the ByTowne), but production was something one had to go elsewhere to do. Film-production activity in the city was either non-existent or sporadic, with Cole, Evanchuk and a handful of others toiling in obscurity. By the late 1980s, even Evanchuk had moved away, although Cole had finished three films in this period. By design, as well as by circumstance, Cole worked in almost total isolation, as Ottawa, unlike most other Canadian cities, did not have a film co-operative. Because of the exodus of aspiring filmmakers to other production centres, Ottawa's film co-op arrived much later than those in other Canadian cities.

In the mid-1970s, the film co-operative movement began in cities from St. John's, Newfoundland, to Vancouver, B.C. The establishment of local co-ops was rooted in an appetite to tell stories on film from the places that produced them. Film co-operatives are locally based collectives in which paid member-ship brings access to cameras, lighting equipment and film stock: the basic infra-structure of filmmaking. Working with extremely low budgets, the co-ops serve as training centres for aspiring filmmakers who, by design and of necessity, work in the auteurist tradition of writing, directing, sometimes editing and even shooting their own films. Virtually every important Canadian filmmaker of Cole's generation (Atom Egoyan, Peter Mettler, Bruce McDonald, Guy Maddin, Patricia Rozema, Jeremy Podeswa, John Greyson, Francois Girard, Gary Burns, John Paizs, et al.) began at a film co-operative. Without these co-ops, it is impossible to imagine the rise of the remarkable Canadian cinema of the last three decades, especially in English-speaking Canada. In a country without a film-studio system or access to its commercial cinema screens, co-ops provide hands-on training and the opportunity to develop personal film styles. In Ottawa, a small band of practicing filmmakers — Cole, Dan Sokolowski, Scott Galley, Monica Szentesky — combined their efforts and secured funding from the federal and provincial arts councils to establish the Independent Film-makers Co-operative of Ottawa in 1992.

Throughout the 1990s, while Cole was either crossing the Sahara or training in his apartment for the coming desert solitude, the Ottawa film-production community began to grow. Through the co-operative, up to ten short films were being produced each year. Most are mediocre, but a number of works began to redefine the staid image of Ottawa. In addition to Cole's unusual films, Dan Sokolowski's live action and animation hybrids lead the experimental side, while Lee Demarbre's freewheeling genre pastiches and parodies of Asian action and blaxploitation films detonate any notions that Ottawa is a lifeless government town.

For most Canadians, Ottawa is an abstraction: the capital, a tourist town, a place to send your taxes and the seat of government corruption. Ottawa is all that, but it is also a border town, where Quebec bristles against Ontario and vice versa; a former lawless lumber town filled with working-class Irish and French who drank and brawled their way out of the nineteenth century; a place where one of Canada's few political assassinations took place; a city where a former prime minister of Canada consorted regularly with prostitutes and spoke to his dead mother and his dog; a place where secrecy and repression strain against insatiable appetites for revelation and scandal. There is even a tourist walking tour of "haunted Ottawa." In many senses, Ottawa is a very peculiar place.

Like Winnipeg's Guy Maddin and John Paizs, who make their strange, imaginative works outside the "centre," Frank Cole's idiosyncratic vision developed in a medium-sized city in the margins of Canadian film culture. His work is at once a response to and an embodiment of the orderly atmosphere of Canada's capital city, unafraid to stare at the roiling fears beneath. Was Frank

Cole Ottawa's Stanley Kubrick? His films were as formally rigorous, challenging and rare as the American master's notoriously infrequent releases. Was he Ottawa's Jean Vigo, who after two masterpieces died prematurely? Cole's films, too, are poetic and unforgettable and he also died young. Of course, Frank Cole was neither and he was both. He was also one of the most remarkable filmmakers to be found anywhere, and was critical to the development of independent filmmaking in Canada's capital. His talents were prodigious; his aesthetic, demanding; his creativity, astonishing; his integrity, indisputable. Indeed, the power of his work is as undeniable as it is difficult to define. One cannot look at the world in quite the same way after seeing a Frank Cole film.

Kill him, they might have whispered in a nocturnal desert language. The ones who would deliver death and disappear into the primal night. Not a second thought. Shred his time on earth and wrap it over our shoulders. His campaign is complete. We will go on. He is fuel for us now. Kill him.

"Frank Cole cannot be with us tonight because he is somewhere in the Sahara desert," I said to the small audience gathered at the Canadian Film Institute's retrospective of Cole's work in November 2000. It was the premiere of his latest feature, *Life Without Death*. I said, half-jokingly, that it was somehow appropriate that he wasn't here, because one rarely sees Frank even when he *is* in Ottawa. He's always been away or else in his apartment practicing the occult arts of solitude. Unlike the last screening of *A Life* at the institute, with Cole in attendance, there would be no achingly long and awkward pauses in his introductory remarks; no unsettling brandishments of longevity magazines or dietary and pill regimes to prolong life; no audience members squirming uncomfortably and staring in mute shock at the intense, gnomish figure preaching with such conviction. All we had that night was the film, and that was appropriate, too, because, perhaps more than any other Canadian filmmaker, Frank Cole was embodied by his work.

As it turned out, Frank was no longer in the Sahara. While I was making my remarks, Frank Cole had been dead for a few weeks and his remains had been returned to be stored, as per the instructions in his will, in a cryogenic tomb in Detroit. The retrospective was, unbeknownst to me, already a posthumous one. There were some in the audience that night who already knew, but they kept it to themselves.

Silence. What is it that cannot be spoken in the sounds of those not speaking? Having been raised Catholic, I understand that silences are never empty. Here was another demonstration. Like waiting for Frank to finish a thought, to return the conversation to my rhythm, to allow me to accelerate, to dismiss me from his spartan enclosure of sonic caesura.

Andrei Tarkovsky once argued that the aim of art is to "to prepare a person for death, to plough and harrow his soul, rendering it capable of turning to good." There is no better encapsulation of Frank Cole's art and his affirmative life as a local filmmaker. We are better because he was here, and diminished by his demise on yet another desert odyssey. What was he looking for out there? Life? Death? It is difficult to say. What *A Life* and *Life Without Death* suggest, however, is that what Frank Cole perceived in the vast, shimmering landscapes and silences of the Sahara were the outlines of his own mortality, the contours of his own harrowed soul and the obscure nature of time itself. Those perceptions found extraordinary expression in his cinema.

The cinema of Frank Cole remains with us. His four films reveal a brave artist who gave cinematic shape to the profound solitude we experience in time, in life and, one conjectures — as one imagines Frank did constantly — in death. The inevitability of death. The adamantine logic of which he tried to outrun, to "beat death just a little bit." His films speak of and to an unavoidable ontological mystery: they seek death out, they search for it. In many senses, their murdered creator embodied it. Now that he is virtually completely disembodied, the mystery of Frank Cole and what he was searching for remains. And we are left with the remains of that mystery. Images. Sounds. Silence.

How

Frank Cole

I'll start to cross the 3,500 miles of the Sahara desert by camel in July 1989. My film about it will be called *Death's Death*. Nobody has succeeded completely crossing the Sahara by camel. To try to learn how, I went to the Sahara to do a 250-mile ride.

October 28, 1988

After I arrived last week I stayed with camel shepherds and walked with them and their camels to a well and back. My thermometer read 102 degrees F in the shade. Coming back, one of the shepherds sat down and fell asleep. I was dehydrated too. We ran out of water. I was seriously dehydrated when we got back to camp. We'd walked one day. Riding across the Sahara will take about 200 days. Two days later I became so sick that I couldn't really walk. I lay down and asked: "How can I cross the Sahara?" What I said next hurt me more than anything ever has. "I can't."

November 27

I prepared for crossing the Sahara by studying first aid, nutrition, bodybuilding, navigation, Arabic. I learned to cope with isolation. For four years. To waste life is suicidal.

I got on my camel about 5 p.m. and my guide and I left Magta Labjar and started this ride. Our camels are carrying about 200 pounds each and they trotted for the next two hours. How do they survive? How?

November 28

When we stopped at sunset I drank a bowl of powdered milk. After such thirst I knew that even if there was nothing else in life than milk … it was enough for me.

November 29

Our camels trotted almost all day. While I rode I watched his camel's legs. Its massive thigh flexed and then held against a step weighing 1,000 pounds. I looked higher up to my guide's legs. His calves are like a bodybuilder's. Though I'm a bodybuilder, his calves are stronger than mine. Sid' Ahmed ould Breibimatt is forty-five. He has the kindest voice I've ever heard. "*Kes,*" he says, as he gives me a glass of tea. He makes me the second and the third. I get into my sleeping bag. His voice will wake me in the morning saying, "*Kes.*"

November 30
When we ride I often repeat this Sahara proverb: "Three things chase away sadness: water, grazing and sympathetic faces."

December 1
I was tired by mid-morning. We were both tired. When we made our morning stop we didn't speak we were so tired. We sat still, drinking tea. We waited for the tea to work. Then we rode on. We were strong again. By lunch we'll be exhausted.

Before lunch we rode into a village called 'Elb Adres and stopped at the well. A man held my hand affectionately. People helped refill our water skins. People spoke to me encouragingly. A man shook my hand goodbye over and over. We rode on. I waved to three women and they waved back, then giggled, embarrassed by their immodesty. I waved to them again and up went their hands. As I rode by a boy, we asked each other how we were. He walked with me a little and then he let out the happiest laugh I've ever heard. I burst out laughing and swung around. I saw everybody again. I wasn't exhausted now. Sympathetic faces had chased that away.

December 2
A circle of kids escorted me through Boutilimit's streets to buy my supplies taking turns holding my hands. Then they escorted us far away. I shook hand after hand goodbye. Girls broke Islamic rule and gave me their hands too. When we were far away I turned around with my camera. The kids ran toward us and let out a whoop that would chase away anything!

December 3
"Kes."
 I sit up in my sleeping bag and thank him.
 "*Shukran. Sid' Ahmed zain?*" (Well?)
 "*Zain. Frank moujour?*" (Sick?)
 "*Frank zain.*"

My cold isn't as bad as yesterday. I have lice but they don't stop me from sleeping. I cut myself from my saddle five days ago and though it opens every time we ride, it hasn't become infected. I have parasites but the recurring nausea hasn't come back since the 23rd. Then the daily start signal comes because Sid' Ahmed has found the straying camels. I hear a long groan.

December 4

Are we lost? This morning when I checked my compass I saw Sid' Ahmed was going further south than my map indicated. In a hundred times I'd compared my compass with his guiding, this was the first time they weren't identical. One of us was wrong.

A few hours later he pointed in two directions, saying he didn't know which we should take. I knew he wanted me to confirm one of the two with my compass like we've enjoyed doing like teacher and student so many times before this. "*Man arrif,*" I said. "I don't know." I didn't know where we were. Suddenly he pointed northwest saying the village's name. He pointed to it but I saw nothing. We rode northwest. About a mile later we rode up to what he'd seen. It was only camels grazing. We made our lunch stop. It was time to treat our routine exhaustion.

Sid' Ahmed made our fire and started heating a bowl of water for my powdered milk. Then he left to ask the owner of these camels for directions. I saw his face was more strained than ever before. I drank a few bowls of milk and ate a lot of dates.

I knew we would run out of water later today. My thermometer was broken but I knew it was about 95 degrees Fahrenheit in the shade. From this high dune I saw nothing all around as far as I could see. The fire went out and Sid' Ahmed still wasn't back. If we changed directions the "route de L'Espoir" road across Mauritania was south about a day or a day and a half. Could we make it?

Then Sid' Ahmed came back. He had directions and we were almost there. I made sure he drank a lot of milk. I tried to make him lie down. "*La bas?*" I asked. (Are you okay?) And in my heart of hearts, I was sorry I wasn't lost. Because I still hadn't learned the answer to my question: how?

December 5

I got into my sleeping bag for the last time on this trip. Often when I do this I think about a little girl called Daat who sang a song for me which is intended to protect the sleeper from death. But this evening I felt something I've never felt before. I wished I was the father of that child.

Yesterday evening when it was time to stop, I rode behind Sid' Ahmed toward a bed of sand. He chose it because of its softness and because it had a bush that provided shelter from the wind. He checked it for scorpions and snakes and then covered any fallen thorns with sand. He laid down a ground-sheet for my sleeping bag... like a father putting a child to bed. This was how. This was how, I realized. This... was how.

And now that I had learned how to cross the Sahara I wished... If only these people's hearts were combined with my people's technology, nothing would be impossible. Even death would be cured.

Short Ends

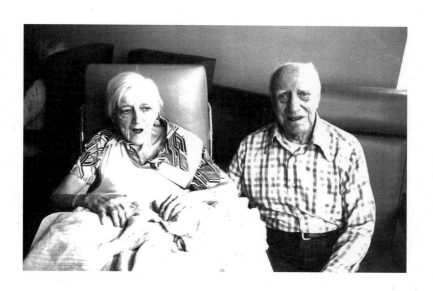

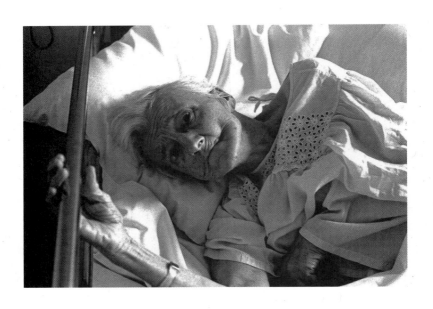

Engravings
Jean Perret and Mike Hoolboom

In order for him to begin, to make a picture, Frank Cole first needs to invent the cinema in a gesture of absolute radicality. He invents true histories that are his alone to see, rooted in a terrifying refusal, and from which he can at last conjure himself with the aid of his camera double.

In his first two short films, he uses his voice to call from the other side of the abyss of representation, asking his subjects to join him in the necessary trial of reproduction. In *A Documentary* (1979), he approaches his grandfather with his voice, in a gesture that allows him to enter a primal scene of trauma, to look at exactly what he can't bear to look at. Standing in front of the last forbidden door, he asks a question that permits entry. Once inside, he invites an epitaph from his grandfather. Every speaking is always the last word, every line might be chiselled into graveyard stone. His voice is also audible in *The Mountenays* (1981), where his beautifully simple questions are put to a family busy becoming pictures, and who are called to accompany this task by Frank's voice. He meets them in order to create a portrait, a moving family photo, which is composed little by little when the last personages and even their dogs enter into the field of looking and take their pose.

Frank's body, which appears again and again in his movies, is also a way of looking. He moves alongside his grandfather, who accomplishes the daily ritual of visiting his wife. Frank is a tender witness available in the time of their common life, which he follows until it is exhausted in a final, noiseless reckoning. He finds his own death there, in the death of his grandfather, and then undertakes a journey of spectacular risks to exorcize his death feelings. His progression in the desert accompanies the ghost of his grandfather. Here the film director works in a space that refuses the separation between the life of a movie and life itself. Each step is part of an approach to find the necessary distance between his subject and himself. He walks in order to put himself into position, again and again, in order to pose the question of seeing. At the edge of exhaustion, when he can hardly go on, the old habits are also fatigued and he can begin to see for himself. This idiosyncratic gesture bears us toward a place of mourning, where the dead are waiting for us. For Frank Cole the way is heavy and serious; here even colours shade into accents of black and white. The work engraves in a twilight aesthetic born of patience and silence. Beauty fades into darkness, arriving only at dusk.

These films are a song of asceticism that draw the field of his solitude and independence. Frank Cole carries his work to the very end of his energies, until he reaches the violent death that is inflicted on him. His immense, monstrous and fussy desire follows each careful step after step, granting death time to work.

It is hardly possible to heal the loss of the social body, but films can help us understand what we've lost and the interconnections between us. The cinema offers us a trace of what was once and a glimpse of the ghosts we are becoming. Refocussed through the director's singular quality of looking, we might again recognize the links of affection that lie between us, the melancholy that some are born into and the marks that lie inside the body waiting to be summoned by a picture's impression.

Beauty is crepuscular. It obtains a collected silence in which one might discern the strained motivations between life and death. The best directors appear and disappear all at once, in the fragile ontology of their pictures. No sooner do they arrive, than disappearance begins. They offer us lyric epiphanies in the authentic voice of silence. Frank Cole disappears progressively in the depth of field of the film narrative that is presented. He grows fainter in the limitless desert, even as he allows us to hear the peculiar silence left to the survivors. In these distant, strained echoes we may perceive the memory of a lost harmony.

Wrecked Cars and Affection
Laurie Monsebraaten

Part One: 1981 Review of *The Mountenays*

"The pure products of America go crazy." — William Carlos Williams

Frank Cole's latest documentary film, *The Mountenays*, brings to mind the opening lines of William Carlos Williams' celebrated poem "To Elsie." The Mountenays are a family of twenty-five living in the woods outside Perth, Ontario, on a lot littered with wrecked auto parts and souped-up jalopies. Here, in a one-room tackboard shack, Mrs. Mountenay feeds and clothes her eleven children on $210.05 a month.

In his portrait of the Mountenay family, the Ottawa filmmaker invites us into the world of these "pure products" of Canada with a sensitivity that allows these people their dignity and lets us share in their simple love for life. Cole's approach is unassuming. The twenty-two-minute black-and-white film opens with Cole's innocuous off-camera questions to Gary, a young adult member of the Mountenay clan. "When do you think you'll have your car out? What will you do?" Gary, who is collecting sap from gas-can buckets nailed to maple trees, replies sheepishly, "Look for some women right off the bat." The scene quickly changes from sap gathering to junk-car racing along a snow-packed country road. Later the men gather in the yard. Gary shows off his prize engine to Cole (who remains always off-camera) and explains the added feature of the instant oil-slick device that can be activated in case of police pursuit. There is laughter and fooling.

Runny-nosed kids and scruffy dogs playing amidst heaps of rusting and discarded auto parts. We might be moved to assume despair at such a scene, but Cole manages to evoke feelings of gentleness and warmth. Life for the Mountenays is a matter of fact. When Cole asks Gary whether he put a cow or horse in his car and drove halfway across the country, he replies, straightly, "A pony, a Shetland pony."

Cole said the idea for the film came to him when he heard about a family that had been ordered by the health inspector to finish the floor of their house. The story goes that a cement truck just backed up to the Mountenays' front door and started to pour. They didn't even bother to move the furniture. Meeting the Mountenays, one is caught between a frown and a chuckle. Inside the filthy, one-room shack at mealtime, we listen to Mrs. Mountenay speak of the welfare department wanting to take her children away. We see an older toothless

Mountenay eat his dinner on a rusted oil drum. But outside in the snow we are reminded of the powerful Mountenay vitality. We smile at a couple of the Mountenay boys attempting to ski, and laugh as Gary raises snorts of glee from the family pig by scratching its ears.

It could be argued that the film lacks a strong focal point, some singular event to startle and grip audiences, and that the film is too relaxed and subdued. This could be directly related to Cole's restrictions with his subject. He admitted he had difficulty with Mrs. Mountenay because she refused to be filmed. In the end, she would agree to speak on tape only about her experience with the welfare department. But because of such restraints, Cole has purposely chosen a quieter development, leaving the Mountenays themselves to win us over without theatrical dramatics. Perhaps the film's finest achievement is that it doesn't try to make a heavy-handed social statement around the Mountenays' story. It is refreshingly free of any middle-class social concern for their way of life. Instead, Cole's film speaks with affection, hope and love.

Part Two: 2008 Review of *The Mountenays*

After writing about social-policy issues as a reporter for the *Toronto Star* for the past twenty-five years, I am struck by how Cole's camera records the Mountenays' poverty and substandard living conditions without judgment. Viewers feel neither empathy nor anger toward the family or the social conditions in which they live. And while there are clearly funny moments, there is no ridicule. The camera simply documents a curious existence.

Among the many lovely moments in the film I didn't mention in my earlier review that stand out for me now is the scene where an adult son plays the board game Trouble, apparently by himself. With the ashes of a lit cigarette dripping from one hand, he punches the plastic bubble that shakes the dice and gleefully marches his marker around the board. It's a striking metaphor for the family's unusual life together in the backwoods northeast of Ottawa, where they are seemingly oblivious to the cares of the outside world.

The family singalong is another scene that draws me in. With one of the children at his side, another brother on guitar attempts a painfully off-key rendition of Elvis's "Love Me Tender." The whole family chimes in later with a rousing version of Charlie Pride's "Crystal Chandelier." Sung with much levity in the Mountenays' country shack, the song about a penniless lover who was dumped by his society girl "for the gaiety of the well-to-do" feels almost autobiographical. The chorus could be the family's theme song: "But will the timely crowd/

that has you laughing loud/help you dry your tears/when the new wears off/ your crystal chandeliers?"

The final scene, as three generations of Mountenays and their various dogs assemble outside in the melting snow for a family portrait, suggests Cole knows this is a film for posterity and a unique snapshot in time.

Nothing to Do With You
Mike Hoolboom

I knew Frank Cole from his desert movies, the long dry solo encounters, the broken flesh and stark beauty, but there are two black-and-white shorts, dating back to his days at Algonquin College, that laid the basis for all that Saharan heat. Like so much of the Canadian fringe, both are family pictures, home movies. The first he named *A Documentary* (9 minutes, 1979) and it pictures with a stunned precision the decline of his grandparents in an old-age home. There is a grief in these pictures so hot it burns to the touch, but it shows itself in the slightly-too-far-away framings that turn his beloved grandparents, and particularly his grandfather, into an element of architecture. The failing flesh, the knotted hands and spotted limbs — this is where Frank learned how to create a frame. The borders that secure each picture are designed to exclude first of all, ensuring that only the strong survive. And once he has cut a rectangle out of his own blood, he steps inside so he will be forced to look only at what he can't bear, only at what he is required, as a duty, to turn away from. This would become the template for all his work.

Every frame in *A Documentary* opens the wound of his stare like a surgeon, deliberately and meticulously. At last, we make a terrible walk down the last hallway on earth to a room where his grandmother lies in bed, moments away from death, and we are made to watch as Grandfather holds this almost-human in his arms. The camera is set behind the bed stand, looking at them the way an interior decorator would size up wallpaper or rug patterns. Unbearable. Grandfather's face looks back into Frank's face, and all of the anonymous watchers he has gathered inside his camera, and he doesn't have to ask why. How can the end be so long? Death lurks on both sides of the screen.

This moment became Frank's home, which he dutifully carried on his back in two long movies made in the desert. But before that he collected his second student short, every bit as powerful as his first, but composed in a different tone altogether. It is called *The Mountenays* (22 minutes, 1980) and initially appears as a kind of anomaly in his oeuvre. It's as if Frank hoped to counter the spell of his dead grandparents by reconvening a family of endless vitality and invention, determined that every frame would erupt with an undeniable life.

And he can't wait to get started. He offers us no preparatory moments or establishing shots, never mind the slow introductions of another life — all this has been left behind. Instead a young man appears in a skeleton of a forest carrying a bucket — winter-coated and bare-headed and already on the move.

One after another, he empties the recycled containers hanging from trees into his bucket, carrying the load of their sweet maple sap, before walking over to the next trunk. But there is something in the way he performs his chore that doesn't make it look like work at all. He doesn't have the efficient walk of an adult accustomed to figuring, at every moment and without end, the shortest distance between two points. Geometry has never occurred to these feet; they are built for wandering, digression and play. The bucket tilts sideways and he looks unconcerned. If some sap spills (though none does), that's okay, there is always more where that came from. What a world of abundance; even the trees are filled with sweetness.

A pair of cars slide across a snowy road while shouts of glee rush from the driver's seat. Happy to be in movement, there's no destination needed — they find again in speed a forgotten tenderness.

In the next scene one of the two cars is parked by a morass of broken auto parts. The hood is open and Frank asks, "What are you doing now?" (The director, always off-screen, never hesitates to become part of the scene. He understands there is no way to be neutral and underlines his complicity with rehearsed, straight-man banter.) With the engine running, the young man explains that he wants to replace the engine he has with a bigger one. But when he reaches into the guts of the machine, he receives a shock and jumps away, a moment that is played for laughs (the truth is, he likes the camera and the attentions of this earnest young director).

Four brothers are also working on cars in what appears to be a wasteland of car ruins. Heaps of tires and body parts and abandoned vehicles are scattered in a forest setting as the brothers aim for more speed. A truck engine guns and pops, and each time it does, one of the brothers jolts as if he were part of the same nervous system. Part junkyard car, part country-life boy. Is that thing going to explode? The boys back off discreetly and leave their comrade firing up the engine, still in search of the perfect ride.

They look like children with their floor-of-a-world strewn with toys. Though everything is oversized, including the children themselves, who appear suspiciously like adults. And instead of toy-store miniatures, remnants of real cars lie broken and discarded at every turn. Wearing a checkered worker's shirt and torn jeans, Ralph throws down metal slabs and tires. "What are you doing, Ralph?" Frank deadpans. "Cleaning the place up," says Ralph in an unintentionally comic reply. He might as well be standing in the ocean announcing his intention to empty it a glass at a time.

Smaller children play in the car graveyard, and then we are led inside a single-room dwelling, home to all twenty-five members of the Mountenay family. Every scene inside necessarily belongs to groupings and congregation. Dinner preparations are underway, and then they sit down to eat. Somehow, there are always enough family present to defeat the intrusion of the camera. It is still there and artificial lights augment the shine coming through the windows, but there are so many busy hands that life refuses to freeze up and wait for the camera to leave so they can be a family again. The animals are there, too, lending their grace and unconcern, a menagerie of dogs and cats hopeful for an extra spoonful, which always comes.

What a tangle of conversations all at the same time. And the camera right alongside.

They wrestle and smoke and comb their hair, stopping every now and then to cast big smiles over to brother or sister. When I see these young, doughy faces stretched into joy, I can't help wanting that too. I want to lean into the picture and take these smiles and cover my face with them, knowing at the same time that they are part of a familial code, a bloodline and inheritance and daily living I will never understand, not even if Frank's movie ran a thousand days long. The happiness each expresses creates a light in their faces, and it is with this light that they illuminate each other, and create their family. Perhaps this is putting it too simply. Perhaps I also have to add poet Anne Carson's observation that every wound gives off its own light. Whenever these faces decompose themselves, whenever they are relieved of the mask of personality and the duties of presentation, whenever they give themselves over to the small revolution of a smile, they are also showing a wound. Every smile opens the face, and this opening is also a cut, a separation, a hole. Which doesn't make me want them any less. On the contrary.

Mother is a large, dominating figure (she is the horizon, the beginning and the end), seen only in glimpses, orchestrating the background. Her long voice-over rap describes a visit from Social Services, who tried to take her children away. Strangers arrived one day from "Toronto," a word she pronounces the way one would name a distant asteroid. "I said, 'As long as my kids have got food in that house and a roof over their heads and they're warm, they're nothing to do with you.' And we've plugged along ever since."

The man-boy in the silver jacket laughs and walks through the chicken coop in a choreographed moment. "How many chickens do you have, Ralph?" Ralph makes Frank repeat the question, though he's heard it perfectly well. While Frank asks again, Ralph preps his reply. "Ten," he barks, looking into the camera with an accusing stare. Why is he so mad? He kicks a chicken. "How many geese?" asks Frank, still sounding like an astronaut. "Two geese and two ducks," answers Ralph straight-up. Then he quacks like a duck with a mimicry so perfect I have to scan back and forth over the scene to make sure the sound is really coming from him. He smiles; the bad moment has passed, the accounting is over. "Can you show us the rabbit?" Frank asks him, and Ralph walks right over to the rabbit hutch. But when we see him again he's wearing a different coat, on another day. The animals move in every direction. Ralph pets a pig. This is how quickly one day becomes another. Ralph is a little soft on the figures — maybe he never picked up the habit of counting — but he knows where that pig likes to be touched all right. And even though the silver running through the camera is too precious to be rolling hour after hour, and it's clear there is something choreographed, nearly rehearsed, in these moments, the man-boy Ralph is still in his animal body; the camera doesn't make him any bigger or smaller than he really is. He's busy living dreams no one reckoned the words for and then it's time to scratch the pig. Two ducks and ten chickens and no one asked how many rabbits. They don't write scripts like this because what is on display, what is at issue here, can't be written down.

A blond Mountenay boy explains why he prefers to live out here: no rent, no cops. And you can drive without your lights on. This conversation, these lives, seem to be conjured out of a forgotten world beyond the flow of capital (there is no one busy buying or being sold). No one from outside is inside — the Mountenays live in a borrowed forest, only too happy to be abandoned and left behind.

Every look and word and gesture tells me again: this has nothing to do with you. Nothing.

At night they play cards and roll cigarettes and sing an off-kilter version of "Love Me Tender." And then a slow, strummed singalong where all the kids chime in. The ones who don't know the words hum along and that's just fine too. You want a little music, you pick up the guitar and learn some, or croon along with sisters and brothers. No sales agents, no deals or downloads. Someone adjusts a light bulb and the screen goes dark.

In a single shot lasting nearly two minutes, the family slowly gathers outside for a group portrait. They exhort off-screen members to join them as they stand shuffling and joking. But wait: those young children held in large wintered arms. Are they the result of sisters and brothers? Or fathers with daughters, mother demanding sons? Where have all these children come from? Am I seeing their darkness, or my own?

71

The credits appear superimposed on a striking image: one of the Mountenay boys is turning a large screw into the ice, moving his body in a slow, winding circle. How beautiful and futile this appears, and us alongside him, our hopes and strivings to make our own special hole so that we can frame infinity with the sum of our fears. His brothers join in, one at a time, and then someone lowers a pole and begins to fish. It is still snowing, but the fisherman has no gloves, he's used to the outside. He's lived out here all his life. He catches a large bass and then another. They call out to Frank, naming him "Frankie." Close, they're getting closer all the time.

Frankie's out there waiting in the cold, too, he doesn't mind. Beneath the ice, the fish are invisible. Beneath their poverty, their backwoods dress and expressions, this family is also invisible. But Frank never sees this. He doesn't know how to turn them into characters and story arcs. It just never occurs to him. Instead, his own loneliness accompanies them and allows him, again and again, to find the right distance when setting up his camera. Not too close, not too far. Here is the magic of this short, beautiful film: if anyone else arrived, they would turn their cameras on, and the family would vanish. Even the animals would be missing. The forest would be empty, the shack house abandoned. Frank's arrival makes their arrival possible.

But this conjuring feat is exhausting, and in his two ensuing features Frank would dedicate himself instead to the art of disappearance. He would use his camera to make everything around him invisible. How well he succeeded, this stern magician and home-movie artist.

Throughout *The Mountenays* he hovers at the threshold of the frame, calling out, asking questions. He wants to know what it's like "in there," in the abyss of representation. Soon he would find an answer to his question by stepping into the arena himself, his own best subject. His next two films largely focused on images of himself, though as anyone who has watched them can attest, he is not there. The Mountenays taught him how to disappear, and he would soon leave for the Sahara, where he could work this magic on himself.

A Life

Frank Cole's *A Life*
Greg Klymkiw

In the seemingly cold world of Frank Cole's *A Life,* one finds a visual virtuosity and emotional core so seldom attained in our country's film industry that I do not hesitate to rank this stunning new feature alongside Vigo's *L'Atalante,* Clement's *Forbidden Games* and Bunuel's *L'Age d'Or* as a work of uncompromising genius. As Cole himself states in his promotional material, *A Life* charts "a man's survival amidst death in a room and a desert."

In the early stages of the film, we are faced with the grainy black-and-white images of an old man. Off-camera a voice (undoubtedly Cole's) asks, "Are you afraid of dying, Grandpa?" The old man, quivering and moist-eyed, seems somewhat perplexed, perhaps even intimidated by the camera. His reply is in the negative, yet somehow it seems inconclusive. Toward the end of the film, the same grainy black-and-white assaults us with an old woman, lying on her deathbed, gasping for life while a voice-over pleads, "Live!" These gut-wrenching, disturbing images bookend a journey that — in spite of the bleak, barren, sometimes horrifying sequences that populate the film — is extremely life-affirming.

In the first section of the film, Cole focuses upon the interior environment of the film's central figure (himself). Moving oddly framed, inanimate objects out of the eye of the camera, the man appears to be ridding the spartan room of what little it has in it. As well, Cole assails us with a variety of strange images: a bare, white wall with a nail driven into it, a phone call that never really comes and is never really answered, a woman with a gun stuffed in her panties and a little girl who runs through plate glass (at first silently, but then followed by the excruciatingly painful sound of the smashing glass). These images are punctuated by recurring shots of the man chiselling, hammering, measuring and planning. He appears to be building something in this barren interior: a room, perhaps? Maybe so, for the man never appears to leave this environment.

But then he leaves one tomb for another. One of the first exterior shots in the film is a series of head-and-shoulder freeze frames of Cole as a variety of backgrounds flicker behind him. It's as if the camera itself is sealing this man in a cold, barren crypt. Yet later on in the film, a voice-over proclaims, "I did this to feel alive." Perhaps the very process of making the film is what keeps the man (the artist) from pulling the same trigger of the same gun that in an earlier scene is used by a woman who appears — ever so briefly — to writhe about and shoot herself in the eye.

And survive she does. The man puts himself through the most rigorous paces in the interior shots and then puts himself (the filmmaker) into the middle of the Sahara desert, where he risks his life to provide a series of stunning exterior images to parallel the equally claustrophobic interior sequences. In the room, for example, we witness a snake slithering helplessly and aimlessly across the hardwood floors, while in the desert, we see Cole himself crawling helplessly along the grains of endless sand. In the room, we hear the sound of wooden matches being struck and eventually extinguished as the snake slithers over them, while in the desert, we see a jeep being doused with gasoline and set on fire as the camera slowly and gradually pulls away, the jeep a flickering speck on the infinite horizon of the Sahara.

The landscape of both the interior and exterior environments of the filmmaker are painstakingly etched to create an overwhelming sense of despair. Even the landscape of the filmmaker's body and head is examined by the camera (or filmmaker's) eye. A less-gifted artist could be charged with mere self-indulgence. Yet Cole's vision is so daring and psychologically complex that by turning the camera on himself in this unsparing manner, he almost creates a distorted image for (and of) the viewer. Allowing this series of terrifying, lonely and some-times beautiful images to wash over oneself is to open up emotionally to a cinematic world that cries for some sense of understanding and passion. This is a sparsely populated world Cole has created, and since the camera is aimed directly at himself, A Life is filmmaking at its most daring and revealing.

The film's emotional core comes from Cole's sadness and desperation, yet one leaves this experience with a sense of fulfillment, a sense that there is life beyond the mere survival Cole painfully explores. This is a film of lasting value and Cole must be commended for the bravery of his vision. As well, it must be mentioned that Jean-Yves Dion's desert photography, Carlos Ferrand's interior photography and Vincent Saulnier's sound design are of a level and quality so far beyond anything seen in recent years that A Life represents some kind of culmination in the world of independent Canadian cinema.

One hesitates to bandy about such words as "masterpiece" in describing anything, but A Life comes about as close to it as anything this writer has seen in some time. And time, as always, will declare the final verdict. A Life seems destined for enshrinement in the history of Canadian film.

Candid Camera
Frank Cole

A Life is my first feature drama: it is about being a man. The film has two locations: a room and a desert. This is a record of a shoot in the Sahara. In 1981 I drove across the Sahara. I returned to Canada and wrote the screenplay in two years. In 1982 I drove to South America to location scout for a correct desert and to take still photographs that form one scene. There is no real desert in North America. In late 1983 the room shooting of *A Life* was completed in a set in Ottawa. In March 1984 I began the desert shooting in the Sahara.

The room shooting finished, cameramen, equipment and financing quit suddenly before the Sahara. A twenty-two-year-old, Jean-Yves Dion, became the single cameraman, the National Film Board in Montreal reversed a decision and became equipment supplier, my grandfather Fred Howard donated the balance of the budget for the Sahara shoot. I filmed him in a coma the day I left. I felt like dying when I saw him.

We passed security control at Montreal because they didn't know what the scorpion was that Dion carried for me in his pocket. We had to laugh.

In Paris I rented a car and drove to Marseilles, then ferried to Algeria. The equipment was confiscated on arrival in Algeria. This was despite introduction letters I had for this situation from the NFB, Canada Council and the Algerian Embassy. In 1981 in Algeria my passport had been arbitrarily confiscated. I was escorted 400 kilometres to police headquarters in Tamanrasset. The equipment was released a day later by mistake.

Government authorization is compulsory in order to film in Algeria. The Algerian Embassy in Canada, after consulting its government, was instructed to issue me with visas. The government authorization itself can be applied for only after arrival in Algeria. There is also no guarantee of authorization. I knew this. I waited three days at the Ministry of Culture in Algiers until the director agreed to see me. Algeria prefers that there be no foreign filming. The fact that I did not want to film people or cities was my advantage. I was given the authorization paper.

I drove a first circuit of the Sahara to find the locations. A nineteen-day drive. I drove the circuit a second time for the shooting. 17,000 kilometres.

We lived in the desert during the first circuit. Temperature at night drops 50 to 60 degrees Fahrenheit from the temperature at midday. I slept cold. Water is generally bad: slated or filled with magnesium or sulphured. One is always thirsty, always. Driving in certain regions requires choosing tracks in the generally correct direction. There is always the risk of choosing the wrong tracks and driving until the gasoline runs out. I did this in 1981 and back-tracked out. There is no exact map of the Sahara.

We lived in hotels whenever possible during the second circuit. This saved us for the shooting. Endurance of the heat and kilometres is evidenced by our rare excretions: the body uses everything.

I risked shooting without a four-wheel-drive vehicle because of financing. This meant being routinely stuck. In 1981 I was stuck on a prohibited and there-fore untravelled site. The car was freed the next day only because of the slight hardening of the sand during the cold night. I drove a Peugeot because of its front-wheel drive and its reputation in the Sahara for endurance. The car endured lost brakes, complete power failures, damaged suspension and lost alignment.

We had one camera and no backup. Sand was the foremost risk. There is always sand in the air. Dion made a cape against the sand that he always dressed camera and tripod in. We used an Arriflex ST for endurance. Film stock was stored in a plastic cooler that was opened at night for refrigeration. I use no sync sound in the desert. I recorded with a Sony Walkman Professional. Silence and wind. The final sound in the desert is flies. I use no life in the desert.

I financed the shooting through the black market. This was illegal but neces-sary in order to have the Sahara. This increased financing by three times. We forged our currency declarations exiting the country.

A day. April 27. I get up as always at 5:30. I have dreamt my grandfather has died. I do not know Gramps has truly died on my thirtieth birthday. Jean-Yves is ill again. I drive 500 kilometres. At the final town we stop to drink. The town's water supply is turned off. A person takes us to a communal water barrel. We drink. Another person takes us someplace there is juice. We drink. It is mid-afternoon. We gather our endurance to shoot today's scene. Out there is where the desert truly is. A lifeless earth. When I drove out there four weeks ago, Jean-Yves shut his eyes. I was also afraid. I stopped the car once and got out to control myself. I thought: a person would only come out here to die. I live best here. I understand it here, it's like my room. It's more home than home itself. It's a fearful home, however. The desert can make you want to die. That's my only fear left. It's time now.

I drink a cooking pot of warm water and drive out. There are new corpses, more animals that did not endure truck transport. This time I don't get stuck. I've learned the methods. We find a tire and it is so large we must carry it on the roof. We locate the abandoned car. There are 125 more of them consecutively if you continue driving. We place the tire inside the car to add for smoke when the car is set on fire. I have difficulty knowing what the shooting structure must be. Jean-Yves works out the correct structure using two shots. I edit when I shoot, that's my need. There is little time left. We will have ten minutes to shoot the scene completely: the time between sunset and dark. If there is any error we will wait until tomorrow with our thirst and the flies and each other. We compose the first shot extremely slowly. Then I do it. The car's underbody is hit many times but nothing breaks. Jean-Yves picks up the gasoline and runs to leave it for me at the abandoned car. He composes the second shot while I pour twenty litres of gas over the car and circle around it. I ignite it and step into position. I have told Jean-Yves to prepare himself to leave immediately if the army investigates the smoke and flames. But there are no distant engines, only silence. Jean-Yves is still ill. He shot 30 percent of the Sahara ill. This was courage. He eats nothing for dinner. He gets in a sleeping bag and shuts his eyes again. He hates being here, he's never hated anything so much.

I am the happiest person in the Sahara. Jean-Yves is asleep now. I must wake him tomorrow while it is still dark. There is something he does not know. It was never necessary to shoot here. I drove 700 more kilometres because I wanted a part of this place. To replace the part the Sahara has killed inside me. I pick up a handful of sand and store it in my suitcase.

A Strange Couple
Fred Pelon

Watching Frank's two desert films again was not easy. Of course there is the beautiful photography that inspires travel and a return to the desert, but the film itself is so humourless, so intensely serious and blunt in sharing his frightening narcissism and perfectionism. It is as if I am looking at a portrait of a serial killer who adores his victims. Is that us, the audience, his once and future loves?

His straight-man act is impelled by the misunderstanding that one has to defy death in order to live. He tells the classical story of coming to know death through witnessing the end of a fellow human — in this case, his beloved grandfather. From this spiritual experience follows the longing for the deathless, the not-dying. This quest for the deathless once created great prophets who ventured into deserts inside and out. Frank chose the external desert and brought back a wonderful collection of images, but his choice finally brought about his physical death as well. At the end of his movie he seems to arrive at the same spot where he started.

Instead of seeing the mind as fundamental in finding the deathless, he mistakenly sees the body as fundamental for surviving. He imagines that he is his body. Life without death is very possible, but it is not personal, and certainly not physical. So here we see a confused man, shocked by the full impact of dying and death, making a journey (externally) and crossing hostile grounds, entering the bottom of what used to be an ocean. But the film allows no passage inward, into his internal hostile grounds, this bottomless space where knowing turns in cycles of birth, sickness and death. What we see is a mad being guided by a nomad and getting lost. Where is here?

When he saw his grandfather dying, Frank longed to take his place, and so he did. When the body of his grandfather ceased to exist, he himself became a dying man. Why do bodies begin and end with so little direction? Throughout the film, I see a sensitive, even tender person, who is also a maniac of control. If anything has blinded him and brought him to his violent death, it was this. Unable to see the cause of his suffering, he travelled voluntarily, and with eyes wide shut, to his execution place.

No Man's Land

My own grandfather was, especially in his last years, someone I needed to need me. I made many walks with him, washed him and collected his feces wherever he left it. He would even feed it to the birds waiting below his window. During these years I often filmed him, walking so very slowly or lying down on his bed waiting for the angels to pick him up, freeing him from this old age. Finally they came. Grief can be a very slow death. Seeing my grandfather die slowly at the age of ninety-six, suffocated by pneumonia, too weak to resist, made me long for death myself. Whenever I felt like falling into a depression, I started to dream about lost paradises far away. This time it was the desert that drew me away from the here and now, the external desert that caught my attention. A newspaper article mentioned that Morocco had recently opened a route cutting through the Western Sahara, a former Spanish colony north of Mauritania. Looking closely on the map, I noticed a village with the name Cansado ("tired"). That's what I was: tired of life. There I would go, to this abandoned village in between landmines and poisoned wells due to the war. Surely that would be a perfect place to lose myself.

I travelled to Morocco, and by means of bus and taxi I arrived, after seven days, at the military zone. By that time I had lost my suicidal urgency and long-ing for an adventurous death in the desert and wanted to turn around. But the military did not allow backwards travel. The only way out was through No Man's Land; that's where the village of Cansado was. To return home, I had to leave the occupied zone and travel south, far away from the military checkpoint. I hitchhiked with a convoy into the desert and after a while told the driver that I had to step out in order to return to the occupied zone. By now I was desper-ate to live but was forced to play with my life. The people in the convoy donated sardines, bread and water and left me standing on a pile of sand. I was told that later in the day a convoy would come and take me back into the military zone. I did not dare to walk or move, knowing that all around lay landmines, and I might lose the track leading out. Finally a Land Rover turned up and the passen-gers were astonished. There, in the middle of No Man's Land, on a heap of sand, was a crazy man waving white plastic bags, desperate for life and a journey home-ward. I had completely forgotten about my grandfather. It would take another journey, one that leads through the internal desert, to finally accept his death, to acknowledge dying and death as a fact.

Frank and I had opposite goals, it seems. He wanted to live forever and I wanted to die forever. But we both grieved in desert crossings. If I had met Frank then, we would have made a strange couple. Sadly enough, Frank is dead and happily enough I am alive. Maybe both of us were busy overlooking what we really longed for.

LOW TOLERANCE FOR PAIN. THIS WILL BE CORRECTED. I REACHED UAXACTUN, AND THERE WERE THE USUAL SNAKES.

WHAT HAS INTERESTED ME MOST IS MY LOW TOLERANCE, FOR ILLNESS. 7 TIMES ILL SINCE CANADA. WHEN I LEFT, THEN THERE WAS NOTHING SO COMPLETELY INTOLERABLE AS ILLNESS. NOW I DON'T CARE ANY LONGER.

ON THE HIGHWAY ON THE NIGHT AFTER LEAVING JUNE 23 I HAD A FLASH IMAGE. I WROTE IT DOWN IN THE MORNING. THE IMAGE WAS OF THE DATE BEING OCTOBER, AND THIS TRIP BEING LONG FROM OVER.

I HAVE DRIVEN 11,000 MILES. IT'S ALL I'VE GOT.

DRIVE. EAT. SLEEP. THAT'S YOUR PURPOSE. THIS IS WHO YOU ARE.

I HAVE WANTED TO CONSUME ALL THESE COUNTRIES, THESE CONTINENTS.

AS I WALKED THROUGH JUNGLE TOWARDS UAXACTUN, I THOUGHT: "THE JUNGLE, IS, THE DEVIL." I HATED IT, PERFECTLY. I WANTED TO KILL IT. AND I WANTED TO LEVEL IT TO DESERT. DROP THE FUCKING BOMB ON IT, PULL THE PLUG. NUCLEAR WASTELAND. DESERT.

AFTERWARDS, I UNDERSTOOD MY CARNAL

NECESSITY OF DESERT. WHERE NOTHING
EXISTS; NO HUMAN BEINGS --- NO LIFE
JUST LIKE ME.

I HAVE MISLEAD YOU ABOUT THE JUNGLE.
THE TRUTH IS SIMPLY THAT THE JUNGLE IS
A MAN. THE OCEAN IS A MAN. AND
THAT EXPLAINS AT LAST WHY WE SURF.
MAN AGAINST MAN. IT'S ALL WAR. THERE
IS NO TOLERABLE POSITION BUT VICTORY.

AGAIN THE NIGHT HE LEFT. V. SAID
TO ME IN THE DARK: "LEAVING, FEELS
LIKE ABSOLUTELY .... NOTHING." I KNOW
I'VE TALKED ABOUT COURAGE, AND,
COURAGE MEANS THE STRENGTH TO BE FREE.
THEY HAVE LET US DO WHAT WE WANT
THIS HAS HAD A TASTE, INDEED IT HAS
TASTED LIKE FOOD TO ME.

UAXACTUN WAS NOT CORRECT. THERE WAS
AN INCORRECTNESS ABOUT IT. I LIKED IT
EXTREMELY. UAXACTUN FELT LIKE A PART
OF ME. IT FELT LIKE MINE.

WHEN THE HALT ENDS AND I REACH
MAINLAND COLOMBIA I WILL DRIVE IMMEDI-
THE 6,000 MILES TO TIERRA DEL FUEGO.
THERE IS NO RETURNING WITH THIS CAR

Dead Serious
Geoff Pevere

Frank Cole contacted me sometime during the summer of 1986. He'd finally finished a movie that had been in the works for years, and he hoped I'd take a look at it to see if I might consider showing it at the film festival I worked at in Toronto. It's odd that I remember the conversation so clearly, but I do. I was standing at the window of my second-storey apartment, impressed that Frank had called me there and not at the office. I remember the strained conviviality of his voice, Frank trying vainly to make small talk with somebody he hadn't spoken to in years, while I tried to reassure him that I was happy to hear from him and was looking forward to seeing the movie. He kept laughing a little nervously as we spoke, something he had always done when we talked. Laughing and smiling were not exactly part of Frank's comfort zone, and when he did, you had the sense it was pure counterintuition.

I'd already known Frank a decade by then. When I was a student at Ottawa's Carleton University, Frank had caused something of a stir with a series of photographs he'd taken of his beloved grandfather dying. It was raw stuff: black-and-white images of the old man succumbing in his deathbed, Frank standing by, both in front of the camera and behind. People accused Frank of exploiting the old man's death, and Frank met the accusations in much the same way he met the lens: with that unblinking, in-your-face, Zen-warrior thing he had, as comfortable with the anger and offence he'd whipped up as if it was part of the art itself. Which, come to think of it now, it probably was.

Ottawa was, and remains, a small town, and you could only traverse its rather tight little bohemian circles for so long before hearing about Frank Cole. I'd heard he'd once been a dancer who'd become a photographer, or a dancer who later made movies. I still tend to think of him that way, even though the dancing part of Frank's life probably only consisted of classes an ex-girlfriend of mine told me she'd once taken with him. Little as I knew about dancing, it seemed to fit, especially if you look at dancing as a way of transporting the body to another realm. And Frank, who was possibly the most unnervingly able-bodied person I'd ever met, was always trying to drive his body somewhere else.

For the campus newspaper, I'd written positively about Frank's photos and his right to make them. I think it meant a lot to him, and for the next several years he always seemed happy when we ran into each other. He was especially keen to talk about film with someone he felt (correctly or not) was as serious about the medium as he was, and never failed to bring me up to date on the project he'd been working on for years. Sometimes I wondered whether it would ever be finished. That's one reason I was delighted to get that call.

When his movie arrived, I watched with glued fascination. There was Frank, more or less exactly as I remembered him: taut, transfixed and swimming deeply in his own universe. It was about a man (Frank Cole) recoiling from his own fear of death by preparing to meet it like a car speeding the wrong way with its headlights off. *A Life* (1986) struck me as one of the most cohesive transferals of artist to art I'd ever seen. Make no mistake: it's a strange work. While there seems to be a prevailing storyline about a man meticulously and ritualistically preparing to execute his own oblivion in the confines of his eerily empty apartment, there are also other elements that intrude: images of Frank's grandfather in his last days, a woman alone in an apartment that's either Frank's or decorated by Frank, a man with a beard who appears in a dream and later shows up dead in a desert, a car driven from an underground parking lot and later covered in gas and exploded by a bullet fired by Frank, and a snake in a box that at one point crawls right up between Frank's thighs before being decapitated by a guillotine Frank customizes out of a windowsill.

Strange, yes, but steady as a shark's prowl. As incomprehensible as some of the images and their purpose may be, they all seem to fit. Part of this is the result of Cole's impressive aesthetic command of the entire enterprise — editing, lighting, sound and, above all, the overall tone. But part of it is also sheer conviction: even if you're not certain of the meaning of what you're looking at, you never doubt it means something. At least to the filmmaker, who makes everything in the movie feel like it's precisely where it belongs. *A Life* is a movie you take on faith or not at all.

Austere, obsessive, narcissistic, hermetic and uncompromising, the film is also indisputably the work of someone who had every single image lodged in his head like masonry. Hard to watch, but *hard* in the literal, stainless-steel sense. It is a movie about a person literally sealing himself off from the world (and into his comfortlessly empty apartment) with tools like hammers, nails, duct tape and a handsaw. *A Life* is a movie of sharp corners, seamlessly secured joints and smoothly finished impenetrability. It's a film made with no apparent audience in mind, a monument to solipsism made from the raw material of a mass medium. Watching it, you feel strangely intrusive, no matter how much you know that *A Life* needed to be seen in order to exist, or how much you suspect it would have been made — *had* to have been made — anyway. If it is unsettling for its traces of morbid self-regard, it is also as pure an expression of the man who created it as if it had been yanked from his guts with pliers.

If there's one aspect of Frank's two features that only grows more poignant with time, it's the solitude. These are not only movies made by and about a man alone, their action is the drama of wilful isolation. In *A Life*, Frank is seen in the ritualistic process of constructing a kind of cell for himself, and in *Life Without Death* (2000), he literally walks into the desert, and away from everything.

As a Canadian film maker, Frank Cole produced work that corresponds with a Canadian tradition of troubled masculinity. As far back as *Nobody Waved Goodbye*, *Le Chat dans le Sac* and *Winter Kept Us Warm*, and as recently as many of the films made by David Cronenberg, Atom Egoyan and Guy Maddin, one sees men walking away. Often, it's an exodus from responsibility: family, love, commitment, sexual intimacy. Sex is an especially fraught arena in movies like Egoyan's *Exotica*, Cronenberg's *Dead Ringers* and Maddin's *Cowards Bend the Knee*, a blend of obsession and fear that invariably results in forms of almost rapturously high perversion.

There is no sex in Frank's movies, but there is sexual tension. Galore. Indeed, it's the kind of wire-humming sexual tension that can only come from such a strenuous denial of its release. And denial of the body — its desires, its functions, its very organic destiny — is a fact of Frank's movies. But one can't escape one's organic destiny, any more than one can transcend death, or hope to cross the Sahara desert alone more than once and expect to come out alive. Frank's films take such pathological flight from human contact, they are decidedly out-of-body experiences. Look at the way his camera lingers on the process of Frank's own physical deterioration experienced in *Life Without Death*. It's clinical, detached and ascetic, a weirdly fascinated captivation with something observed, not felt.

Losing oneself in the wilderness is, of course, one of those defining Canadian themes: in this country's quiet mythology, frontiers don't open on horizons of possibility; they open on vast expanses of nothingness. You disappear in them. In this, at least, Frank's films may display aspects of Canadianness that are (typically) pathological in their extremity, especially when it comes to sex, masculinity and the sheer impulse to get as far from human concern as is geographically possible. But that's also why this mythology is so stealthy, and

why it takes a long view indeed to find the proper perspective to put Frank Cole's work in any context other than Frank Cole's work. If the context is solitude, you only fit if you're alone.

One of my most vivid memories of Frank Cole is the way he stood at the front of the auditorium to take questions following the impressively packed Toronto festival premiere. He was dressed in his customary skin-tight, head-to-toe black, and he planted himself dead centre and stared down the crowd like a dare. The room was unusually but unsurprisingly quiet, considering what they'd just seen. Frank entertained those few questions that were asked as though he were tending goal against Russia. If he was nervous, it only showed when that spasmodic smile of his leaked.

Afterwards, he thanked me profusely for what he considered a roaringly successful launch of his movie. I asked him what was in the cards next, and that's when he told me he was probably going to cross the Sahara alone on a camel — a logically illogical follow-through of the promise left at the end of *A Life*. He also said he hoped to make a movie about it. That was the last time I ever saw or heard from Frank Cole.

He did cross that desert, largely alone, and aboard more than one camel, and the resulting documentary, *Life Without Death,* is every bit as strange, accomplished, uncompromising and distinctly *Frank* as *A Life* itself — even more so, if possible, precisely because it's a documentary. Although *Life Without Death* takes Frank out of his apartment and into the world, the ultimate impression is of a world reduced to Frank's vision of it: it is every bit as elementary, predatory and mysterious as the filmmaker's fictional universe, and defined by the same monolithically unforgiving life/death paradigm. If *A Life* at least grants the viewer the possibility that the filmmaker's fixation on seizing life by facing death is merely the stuff of acute artistic inspiration, by the time you're watching Frank actually cross that desert — threatened by bandits, besieged by insects, wasting away to near-nothingness — you know he's playing for keeps. Which is to say, not really playing at all.

Most of the world that saw *Life Without Death* had got word that Frank was dead. He'd gone back to the Sahara planning to cross it both ways this time, and his body had been found tied to a shrub near Timbuktu. All his camera equipment and film had been stolen (and never subsequently recovered) and his camels — tattooed precisely in the event of such a development — were gone. The bandits whose presence he'd been warned about so frequently in *Life Without Death* had caught up with him, and they'd done exactly what he feared they'd do. Needless to say, the news only made the watching of the documentary that much harder.

In preparing to write for this book, I watched *A Life* and *Life Without Death* for the first time since their release. A couple of things struck me. First of all, the extent to which certain images and sounds had adhered themselves to my memory so firmly. Although seen only once — for neither is the kind of film that easily invites multiple immersions — Frank's films had made an indelible impression. Compositions, cuts, camera movements, sounds, the dry monotone of Frank's voice — I realized these things had never really left me, and only needed the reactivating influence of another viewing to leave me with the odd impression that I knew the movies far more than I even knew I knew them.

The other thing that struck me was the finality. Granted this impression is impossible to disentangle from either the pervasive, debatably self-fulfilling, obsession with death that cloaks the films, or from the death of Frank himself. These kinds of things tend to put a rather tight choke leash on one's response. But there's another kind of finality at work in these movies, and it's the finality of Frank's art. As eloquently and distinctly articulated as Cole's two features are, they leave one with very little expectation of their maker's growth as an artist. If anything, Frank's single-minded pursuit of death, both as an object of artistic inquiry and as a personal challenge, may have not only guided his muse but monopolized it — a suspicion only made more substantial by his returning to the Sahara to make yet *another* movie about his great obsession. What could possibly have been left to say? Or did that even matter? Certain questions are therefore inevitable: would Frank ever have moved beyond the need to make movies about his fixation with death? *Could* he have?

These are thoughts that invariably bump up against the possibility of pathology and mental disturbance in Frank's work, questions best left outside a critical appreciation of the films. I guess my point is that Frank's work is almost impossible to disentangle from Frank himself, especially if you knew him. It was clearly his great gift that he was able to make movies that seemed such an organic piece of him. But it may be our loss that this piece was so persuasive. Had there been others, Frank might have taken journeys other than the one that ultimately killed him.

In the Theatre
Mike Hoolboom

Up against another human being one's own procedures take on definition.
— Anne Carson

We never met. Though I heard his name spoken often, by friends and strangers, and always with a slight lowering of the voice, as if they were about to reveal a secret, inviting the listener to lean in close. "Frank Cole ... " they would tell me, and then pause, letting the effect of the words sink in. It wasn't like other names somehow, certainly not like the names of my peers, who were babies, children in the nursery of cinema, bewildered by the need to express longings which for some would never be named at all, even all these years later. But with Frank Cole — no one ever called him Frank, that would be altogether too casual, too offhanded for a young man born serious — the name was already something to aspire to. He had understood before any of us that the only way to make the stories cinema required was to live them first, and his terrifying commitment was enough to lower the tone whenever his name was dropped into the room.

Fall in Toronto means the Toronto International Film Festival, which used to be called, in a moment of breast-beating that seems somehow very un-Canadian, the Festival of Festivals. The long summer is over, and now it's time to reap the harvest, the new crop of pictures gathered from round the world and laid up where we might be able to judge the distance between last year's viewer and the present, trying to hip ourselves to some brave new trick of the light that would make our unaccustomed lives possible again. What we were watching, of course, was ourselves.

And this being a festival in Toronto, there was a requisite Canadian component, tucked away behind more glamorous emulsions. Here were eyes raised in our own light, and if these looks were not the usual, it was only because we'd grown accustomed, like most everyone else in the world, to the multinational musings that continued to occupy our cinemas and imaginations like an invading army. The cinema of Hollywood. But for a breathless stretch in autumn, it was possible to glimpse something else, and it was in search of this strangely familiar that I stood in queue for a new movie by the man whose name I'd heard only in whispers, returned at last to the place of his birth, but not before circum-navigating some lost continent, swallowing miles of the Sahara, beating himself with it, until the two had become, man and desert, inseparable.

The movie was called *A Life* and there are vivid stretches that have lingered long after a thousand other movies have paled. He couldn't stop going, that's what his friends told me. He travelled by jeep, and then went back to do it again on a camel, and then again by foot, crossing the Sahara of his life over and over, waiting for everything to change, and then everything did.

The film I saw was just a few minutes long, though *A Life* by Frank Cole, the movie that showed that afternoon at the festival, was, by anyone else's account, a feature-length endeavour. There were just two scenes in my version of the film: one showed Frank walking the Sahara, while the other offered an unbearable recount of his grandfather's last moments. His home-movie science fictions appeared in black and-white, clipped from a re-view of Frank's first film, *A Documentary* (1979). He returned to this footage like an obsessive worrying the beads, and what he found was not only his beloved grandfather, but death itself. Every black-and-white moment teemed with Swiss shock and outrage. The camera did not observe, it stared. The framings were coolly exact, the white-on-white institutional hallways and waiting rooms provided some further remove so the infernal miracle could take place. As the camera rolled, the man Frank Cole once knew, the grandfather of his youth, disappeared, and in his place stood death itself. This is the guide Frank used to make his way across the desert, which was not a memory, but a living hand showing him where to cross and pitch his tent and place his camera.

The film lasted just a few minutes and then the lights came up and for a moment there was nothing, not even the polite applause that greeted even the most execrable of the festival's offerings (this was Canada after all), and then the programmer, it must have been Geoff Pevere, stood up and announced, "Frank Cole." We were roused from our stupor and began to clap and the clapping lasted a long time, as if we were handing up not for this devastating film, but for ourselves, urging ourselves out of suspension. Then, just as suddenly, realizing what we were doing, in a collective moment of self-consciousness, the applause stopped. There followed nothing but a long and awful silence as Cole stepped away from the tribe, from us, as alone as he would ever be, leaving everyone a little shocked. Because the Cole that we had just watched crossing the Sahara was a lean, browned slip of a man, while standing before us was a great, eerie, bulked-up beast. Frank had obviously been doing some serious time in the gym. His neck, for instance, was now as big as my head, and his arms bulged out of the sleeveless T-shirt he wore for the occasion.

With an entirely affectless sense of drama, he stepped forward until he was standing directly beneath one of the harsh, overhanging floods of the auditorium that turned his face into a Halloween version of itself. Long shadows dripped across the place his face should have been and he smiled in a silence that absorbed everything it touched because after this movie we knew only that whatever the cause of his happiness it was nothing like a happiness we could know. He stood there with those twin beef pillows crossed in front of him, not saying a word, and no one else said a word either. Someone had told me — Lori maybe, or Peter, or Steve, someone who knew him when he was only human — that this movie was going to be called *Death's Death*, but at the very last moment, as the program book was about to shipped to the printer, he'd decided to rename his film *A Life*. I stammered out this question hoping only to hear him break the soundless barrier, and after some lengthy moments of deliberation he said that while finishing the film he realized that dying was a choice. No one had to die. Because the words came out in a flat, even clip, there was never warning his speech was coming to an end, no dramaturgy attached to the rising and lowering of tones that offer cues to the listener. This was a democracy of language, each word granted the same weight and intonation, issued by someone who was mistrustful of speech. He had come to stand before his images, before the light that made his pictures possible, and as a result each of his replies (which were invariably brief) was followed by a long, nearly unbearable silence. This silence was more telling than anything he said, because this was the place Frank Cole must have wrestled his pictures out of. Later, when the last painful question had been asked, everyone made an uncommon rush for the back door as he stood rooted in the footlights. Unmoving, he watched us return to our ordinary catastrophes and begin the long road of forgetting everything we'd just seen. By the time he finished his next film, there would be no invitation to present it at the festival. It was already too late for that. He was found murdered, ambushed by thieves on his latest trek across the Sahara.

It was with sadness, and little surprise, that I learned of his end while flipping through the entertainment pages of Canada's national newspaper. In the days to come, there were conversations with those who had surfed the same coast or sold him a camel. And there were others who had rubbed closer to the bone, those who might have sat and crouched in the same fire. They all said the same thing, the ones who knew him best, and the ones who didn't know him at all. Frank Cole was dead.

The Placebo Singers of Howard Stone

John Greyson

At funerals in medieval France, it was customary for the mourning family to serve food and drink to the congregation. As a consequence, distant relatives and unrelated parasites would descend on the ceremony, performing elaborate displays of simulated anguish in the hopes of a free meal. The practice became so widespread that these hangers-on were dubbed "placebo singers," named for the first word in the first phrase of the collectively sung "Office of the Dead" funeral mass: *"Placebo Domino in regione vivorum."* ("I will please the Lord in the land of the living." Psalm 114: 1-9).[1] Over time, the term evolved in French and English to refer to any sycophant who sought "to please" for some reward, and eventually, to any substance that a well-meaning doctor might give a patient, wishing "to please" her by claiming it as an efficacious cure, when in fact it was no more than a sugar pill. Conversely, *Hoopers Medical Dictionary* of 1881 speculated that any positive effects might be attributed to the subconscious wish of the patient "to please" the doctor by getting better. The fact that remarkable recoveries sometimes did occur following the administration of such sweet nothings was increasingly remarked upon and coined the "placebo effect," returning the term to its musical origins of centuries earlier. The crocodile tears of the original placebo singers might have been mercenary sugar pills, but they nevertheless contributed substance to the spectacle of succour. Their overwrought simulations afforded grief-stricken families a pleasing contrast, a placebic backdrop of artificiality against which to perform the authenticity of their loss.

Howard Stone[2] (played by Frank Cole) is the central character in *A Life*, appearing in almost every scene. His performance is exact and almost silent, a monk who has long ago taken his vows. His room is white and square, and contains a bed, a desk, a window and a snake. He travels by car in the desert, finds a bearded corpse, and nearly dies. His grandparents die onscreen, first one and then the other. Death permeates *A Life*, erupting in staccato bursts that stab at the calm of the elegant compositions, administering jolts.

At Howard's funeral, six placebo singers joined the mourning family, singing of a man they knew only through his film. George Bernard Shaw, attending with his friend T. E. Lawrence, was heard to mutter: "Hell is full of musical amateurs, and brandy is the music of the damned."[3]

Glenn Gould (played by Colm Feore), the first placebo singer, never considered crossing the Sahara, instead seeking his own oblivion on a frozen

Muskoka lake. Walking out to the creaking centre, he would survey the distant shore around him, an insecure perimeter that blurred ice and sky. Glenn would nearly faint from the delicious vertigo, fatally aware that his slight body was perched a hundred metres above the lake floor, that he might fall through a sudden crack, slip down through the black water to join the pickerel slumbering in the mud. Glenn wondered if Frank had ever felt a similar vertigo in the desert, perhaps in a windstorm when the sand becomes as liquid as water, where a car could falter and drown in the dryness, tires sinking like those of his insufficient Peugeot, which he had rented for his Algerian Sahara scenes.[4]

Glenn stood to read his brief eulogy, quoting Frank's favourite desert explorer, Antoine de Saint-Exupéry, author of *The Little Prince* (upon whose eponymous hero Frank modelled his *A Life* costume of perfectly tight pearl-grey pants and perfectly tight pearl-grey shirt framing his perfectly tight pearl-grey buttocks): "What makes the desert beautiful is that somewhere it hides a well." Yet even as he read the words, Glenn wondered whether Saint-Exupéry's words about the ocean might better have captured Frank's exacting approach to filmmaking, to the extremes he extracted from his collaborators: "If you want to build a ship, don't drum up people to collect wood and don't assign them tasks and work, but rather, teach them to long for the endless immensity of the sea."[5]

The Woman from Malibu (played by Colin Campbell)[6] was also a placebo singer at Howard's funeral. She sat at the back, never removing her sunglasses, ignoring the proceedings, remembering instead the way Howard toned his body in *A Life*. Skipping rope, stretching, every gesture succinct and fastidious, the same firm way she applied her lipstick, her eyelashes, pulled on her blond wig. In her mind's eye, she could see scenes from the film again, see his naked body in the shadow of the room. She flinched, remembering, for in the flash of a quick edit, his body became a woman's, with the same thighs and waist but now also breasts, writhing in space, now on the floor, a frenzy.

Howard and the Woman from Malibu both liked barren rooms and harsh sunlight, sharp shadows and the desert. They were different, of course. She wore pink sweater sets, he favoured black briefs. She liked restaurants with a toaster on every table, he had no kitchen at all. For every thousand words she spoke, he would say one. Like for instance: "*alif*," the word for "one," the first letter of the Arabic alphabet, which he tattooed onto his wrist in the middle of *A Life*. He said it aloud, and it sounded like "a life." His tattoo was a placebo, a blue slash standing in for a red wound, the cut of a blade. She thought of the bullet scar on Chris Burden's arm. She thought of Vito Acconci, masturbating under the

floor of his gallery.[7] Semen shooting out of a man, a bullet shooting into a man: a tattoo lingering. When Howard stripped and poured a bucket of sand over his baked body, she shivered, remembering what it felt like to walk out into the eternity of the desert, alone with the platinum sun, in search of pony skeletons.

The two placebo singers in the next row were The Woman (played by Maya Deren)[8] and Jeanne Dielman (played by Delphine Seyrig), the former in black silk, the latter in grey wool. They took off their sunglasses and whispered tersely.

"It's you who should sue, Jeanne. Frank stole your best ideas, the way you filmed bodies in domestic space, the loneliness of a home. The abrupt way he exits frame, just like you and your light switches on and off as you leave rooms. The duration shots where he performs a task, rasping or hammering or waiting, just as you peeled potatoes. He shifts his filing cabinet exactly the way you clean your tub!"

"No, no, you've got the better claim, my dear. Think of his black rotary telephone, the very image of your own in *Meshes*, right down to his gesture of yanking the cord. That's no coincidence, I'm sure. Think of his gun, echoing your knife, his dead body on the floor, echoing yours in the chair. Most of all, think of his shattered window, his guillotine, the shards of glass displayed on the floor, just like yours. Of course, he's reversed the roles: in *A Life*, it's the young girl who flees from him, perhaps a suicide leap out the window, while in yours, it's you who raises your arm to stop your husband, and in the process, smashes the cinema frame itself."

"But, Jeanne, you can't deny, he shot his film in Ottawa, and isn't Ottawa truly the Brussels of North America? When I saw the snake lying on top of him in the bed, stretched thick between his legs, all I could see was you on your back with your last customer. He chokes his snake with one hand, his expression utterly blank, just the way you stab your man to death, staring up at the ceiling."

"But the key is the camera perspective, always third-person, always omniscient: in *Jeanne Dielman* … yes, I'm staring, but it's the camera who is always an observer, staring back at me. In *A Life*, the perspective swaps continually, just like in *Meshes*. It's you that Frank copies, cutting from an omniscient wide angle, to a psychological close-up, to a detailed point-of-view, to a memory of what the character sees or imagines. The pattern is repeated, reversed, then broken, purposely shattered, then a moment later restored. The construction and disintegration of a subjectivity, a body in a box."

"A prison."

"But which prison? The body, the house, the town, the desert?"

"Or each inside the other, like a Russian doll, fitting as tightly as his pants."

"Did you see, Jeanne, how he sipped his gasoline in the desert, just the way you sipped tea in your café on Quai du Commerce? From the looks in your eyes, neither of you are sure whether you're ingesting a placebo or a treatment, a poison or a cure. And then he tasted the sand from the jar with a snake-flick of his tongue, just the way you nibbled your biscuit."

"It's not sand, it's his grandfather's ashes. He drops them on the floor, and then has to scrape them back up, mixed with shards of broken glass. He touches his finger to his lips."

"He hadn't been to the Sahara yet so it couldn't be sand, that scene was filmed beforehand. So maybe it *was* his ashes. But it spills like sand."

T. E. Lawrence (played by Peter O'Toole) ascended the pulpit and read from *The Seven Pillars of Wisdom,* his celebrated memoir of his Turkish campaign during World War 1, the book recognized by some as Howard's constant companion and bible. For Lawrence, the desert was always a covert expedition toward the body of the Arab: "Our youths began indifferently to slake one another's few needs in their own clean bodies … friends quivering together in the yielding sand with intimate hot limbs in supreme embrace, [who] found there hidden in the darkness a sensual co-efficient of the mental passion which was welding our souls and spirits in one flaming effort."[9]

Hot stuff indeed, but for Howard, the desert was the opposite, a site of monastic narcissism, offering a sure escape from the fraternity of modernity. Only one body mattered in the Sahara, and it certainly didn't belong to any Bedouin who actually lived there. Howard offered his body to the camera as an oblation of onanistic renunciation, an ark of homoerotic vanity. The only other actor in his desert, Abderrahmane Ghris, appears briefly in a midnight wet dream, and then again as a corpse, killed by a snakebite or the car, a body that Howard ministers and then abandons, stone-faced. This bearded cameo suggests a Jesus that didn't survive his forty days and forty nights, a Christ that perhaps succumbed to the Devil's sly temptations, agreeing to turn stone into bread and then dying from indigestion. Does this make Howard Stone the devil? In his barren Ottawa room, after he wrestled with his snake, Howard ate an apple. Was this a genuine safeguard against depravity, or the opposite, an Eve-like flirtation with knowledge — or merely a placebo?

Lawrence, captured by the Governor of Deraa, was stripped naked, whipped by guards and then raped. "A delicious warmth, probably sexual, was swelling through me ... "[10] In response, the corporal, the youngest and handsomest of the group, "flung up his arm and hacked with the full length of his whip into my groin." Howard needed no whip, trusting the desert itself to provide the flagellation. Shackled only by the tightness of his trousers, he produces an echo of this warmth for the camera when he wets his pants, the stain soaking the denim and filling the frame.

From the back and naked, Lieutenant Takeyama (played by Yukio Mishima) and Howard Stone (played by Frank Cole) were interchangeable: powerful shoulders and the tight waists of divers, fine black hair on their forearms and thighs. Both followed punishing workout routines, and recorded the results on celluloid, ensuring that all eyes could witness the private moments when they flexed their perfection. Like the set of *Yokuku*[11] (the only film Mishima directed), Howard's room in Ottawa resembles a Noh stage, a space stripped of decoration, where the body is displayed against planes of light and shadow. In honour of Howard's funeral, Takeyama exchanged his white loincloth for a pair of black briefs.

Takeyama spoke: "In the deepest feeling of Japanese, there is a profound concept that the ecstasy of sexual intercourse is identified with the ecstasy of suicide, especially self-sacrifice ... The weight of love and death should be equal in this short film, as if a white column and a red column would support a celebrated lofty arch."[12]

He continued: "I approached *Yokuku* as a placebo, a chance to consume the ecstasies of both columns without necessarily taking the final cure for life. *Yokuku* permitted me to rehearse the rapture of seppuku as spectacle, first as a performer, and then as a spectator, reliving with my celluloid doppelgänger the moment when the sword seems to plunge into my belly, when my entrails seem to spill onto the floor. Howard made *A Life* in the same way, as a sugar pill against the end he feared most, yet equally, as an oracle that would predict his fate: a knife in the belly as he slept alone beside his camel, under the stars. *A Life* rehearsed the end he professed to dread, yet seemed to chase, returning twice more with his camera to the night sands of the Sahara.

"In *Yokuku*, my camera follows the stain of blood dragged across the floor by my beloved, her kimono serving as the pliant brush. Howard crawls from his camera, naked as a snake save for these black briefs, his blood painting the floor in a smear between his legs. We made these films to sit like pills on our tongues, ensuring that all eyes could witness the private moment when we'd swallow, whispering these words: 'Yet each man kills the thing he loves, by each let this be heard; some do it with a bitter look, some with a flattering word; the coward does it with a kiss, the brave man with a sword!'"[13] A tear trickled down his cheek.

A snicker from the back row. "Oh, Mary, put it back in your pants!" It was Glenn Gould (played by Colm Feore). "Surely our Howard doesn't deserve such smarm."

Lawrence (played by O'Toole) chuckled in agreement: "Could be worse, chaps, next our dear Takeyama may start intoning that dreadful chestnut: 'He was my north, my south, my east, west ... '"[14]

Malibu (Campbell) chimed in with illustrative hand gestures, miming the compass points, calendar, clock: " ... My working week and my Sunday rest; My noon, my midnight, my talk, my song; I thought that love would last for ever: I was wrong."

Takeyama (Mishima), sulking, returned to his pew, while the others bickered amiably about the relative merits of Wilde vs. Auden, and the limits of such florid romanticism when applied to an ascetic such as Howard. Thinking about the film as a self-prescribed therapeutic process (one defined perhaps by aesthetic empathy), or at least the simulation of such, they took turns proposing which iconic image might truly be nominated as Howard's signature placebo. For Dielman, it was the window; for Malibu, the corpse; for Lawrence, the campfire; for The Woman, the little girl; for Takeyama, the gasoline; for Gould, the snake.

The lights dimmed and an official announced that the memorial screening of A Life was about to begin. They lapsed into silence, happy to be mesmerized again by the elegant formalism of the shots, the precision of the tempo. Minutes pass, and they settle into their pews, drowsy in the darkness of the afternoon, complacent in their familiarity with Howard's story.

Then: they are shocked by Howard Stone's grandmother. They had forgotten her, forgotten this moment at the nine-tenths mark of A Life, where she appears briefly but changes everything. She has been hovering throughout, an absent ghost, hinted at only by the scarce shards of the grandfather's grief, by the moments when Howard contemplates a photo of himself with his grandfather. Until now, this film has been about two men, a grandfather and a grandson, bonded by blood, the younger performing rituals of abjection in honour of the older. Indeed, the film ends at the grandfather's deathbed, with Frank's camera precisely recording the grandfather's passing. The final words in this almost wordless film are: "Old man."

But then, she interrupts: a few seconds of life, and then, not. Suddenly the elegant games and patterns of the film fall away, leaving a void as vast as the Sahara. She is still. The camera moves around her slowly, handheld. Her eyes are black marbles, her mouth forms a black cup, hollow and cold. She is gaunt and open, grasping for a final word, a final breath. She is in the process of becoming stone, and the film itself is failing, the elegant camerawork starting to falter, the exposure inaccurate, the focus tentative. She is dead, an unequivocal unadorned fact, witnessed at great cost by Cole and his camera, and neither sand nor ashes nor any sugar pill can contradict this certainty.

Notes

1. Nowadays some wags prefer to sing it thusly: "Placebo Domingo likes regional coke'n'rum."

2. Howard Stone is the name several sources cite for the character that Frank Cole plays in his first feature, *A Life*, 1986, half-shot in an Ottawa studio, the other half in the Sahara. However, the credits of the film refer only to the characters Mr. and Mrs. Fred Howard (Frank Cole's maternal grandparents), and do not indicate Frank playing any character. Though Howard Stone and Frank Cole can seem interchangeable, and Cole certainly seems to court this collapse, lurching into documentary and autobiographical tropes at times, it's important to maintain the Howard/Frank distinction.

3. George Bernard Shaw, *Man and Superman*, 1903.

4. Cinematographers have at times chosen to shoot scenes of arctic tundra in the desert, swapping the frustrations of snow for the lesser frustrations of sun, allowing the sand to perform as a placebo. Later in the lab, they colour-correct the tan dunes to become blue glaciers.

5. Antoine de Saint-Exupéry, *Terre des Hommes*, 1939.

6. The Woman from Malibu was a recurring character in a series of six tapes by Campbell. The final one, *Hollywood and Vine* (1977), begins with these words: "I almost ran over Liza Minelli today. I had just got back from Chrome City. I had been to the funeral of an old friend, who had been fumigated to death, accidentally. Her house had termites. She was upstairs when the fumigators came. They sealed off the house, and pumped it full of poison gas. They found her the next day, slumped underneath her hairdryer."

7. Burden's 1971 performance *Shoot*, at F Space in Santa Ana, involved an assistant shooting a bullet into his arm from a distance of five metres. Acconci's *Seedbed*, at Sonnabend Gallery in New York, also 1971, featured a ramp on the gallery floor that concealed a naked Acconci. His masturbatory fantasies about the gallery visitors were amplified through the gallery.

8. The Woman is the central character in Maya Deren and Alexander Hammid's *Meshes of the Afternoon* (1943). A feminist classic, it uses various avant-garde techniques to explore the possibilities of representing trauma and the subconscious. Originally silent, the score was added in 1957 by Deren's third husband, Teiji Ito. *Jeanne Dielman, 23 Quai du Commerce, 1080 Bruxelles* (1975) is

Chantal Akerman's three-hour minimalist melodrama, which uses real-time duration to document three days in the life of a Bruxelles housewife/prostitute. The ennui of bathtub scrubbing is juxtaposed with the boredom of fucking; lights are habitually switched on and off.

9. T. E. Lawrence, *Seven Pillars of Wisdom*, 1926.

10. Ibid.

11. *Yukoku* (*Patriotism, or the Rite of Love and Death*) (1965), adapted from a short story by Mishima and inspired by the Ni Ni Roku incident, tells of an army lieutenant who commits seppuku ("stomach cutting"), following a failed coup. A minor sensation at the time, the film became notorious seven years later when Mishima committed actual ritual suicide, following a botched uprising to restore the powers of the emperor. Suppressed by his widow, the film only became available again in 2006. It's thus improbable that Frank Cole ever saw this film, though he perhaps knew about it, given the widespread publication of still images from it, of Mishima in character. It's very likely that he'd seen *Meshes of the Afternoon* and *Lawrence of Arabia*, and perhaps also possible that he'd seen *32 Short Films About Glenn Gould*, *Hollywood and Vine* and *Jeanne Dielman, 23 Quai du Commerce, 1080 Bruxelles*.

12. Yukio Mishima, "On Patriotism," essay in *Patriotism: The Film* (translated by Ted Goosen), 2006.

13. Oscar Wilde, *The Ballad of Reading Gaol*, 1898.

14. W. H. Auden, *The Ascent of F6*, 1936.

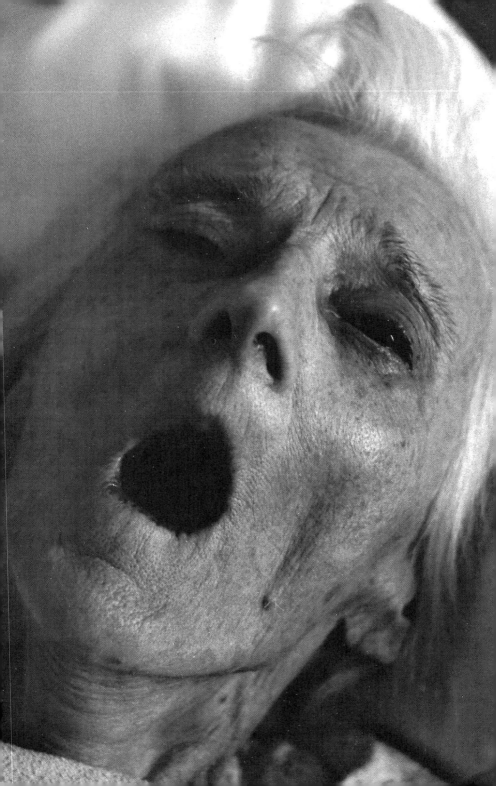

They Called Me Dr. Death
A 1991 Interview with Frank Cole by Gary Nichol

FC: I was born in 1954 in Saskatoon, Saskatchewan, a town we left when I was a baby. Dad joined the diplomatic service ten years later. We moved to Ottawa, but most of my high school was in Switzerland and South Africa because Dad worked there.

GN: Where in Switzerland?

FC: We lived in a town called Montre, which had an international school with English and German sections. I was in the English section for three years and then I went to high school in Capetown, South Africa, for a year and a half. I think the biggest influence it had was… it started to make me a bit of a loner because I hated the school system so I distanced myself from everybody.

GN: Did it occur to you that you might have some creativity in you? Like the old joke that goes: can you play the fiddle, Pat? I don't know, Mike, I never tried. (*robust laughter*)

FC: You're asking me what made me want to learn how to become a filmmaker. I want to have an answer but I haven't figured it out yet.

GN: After your BA, you went to Algonquin College for three more years to learn how to become a filmmaker. Did you look hard at the program or wander into it?

FC: I also applied to the French national film school in Paris but I wasn't accepted. What was best about Algonquin was that with a little determination you could do whatever you wanted. All of the equipment and people and crews were there. We were taught about every area of filmmaking and did short exercises in camerawork, sound and editing. It was a very practical program.

GN: Do you think it's odd that you picked such a public medium, being such a private person?

FC: What I don't like about who I was then was… (*pause*) Self-publicizing was too much a motivation in me.

GN: Really? I didn't think so. I remember you getting in a fight with a girl from the audience at your screening. It was a great battle in front of everyone.

FC: Another word to describe it is "egoism." I was egotistical.

GN: It stood you in good stead because people like our teacher Tonda, who found you unpleasant as a student, now appreciate you, and see how your personality gives a unique bent to the medium. Every Frank Cole film has its own style; it's not going to look like just another documentary film.

FC: I think Tony was justified in disliking me, because I was an egoist. And I think the reason why he likes me a little more now is because I'm not as egotistical as I was. The one advantage I have is that I really don't like egomaniacs, so that should make it a little easier. Self-hate. *(laughter)* You've heard that before.

GN: Was the moment you could get your hands on film fulfilling?

FC: To hold that first film in my hands was everything to me because it gave me a reason for living. I think that was why I started studying filmmaking. I didn't have a strong purpose in my life.

What struck me most about going to film school was the general difference between other students and myself. Most of the others cared about marks and I didn't care at all. The only thing that mattered was having a film by the end of the year. I think I just happened to be somebody who has never looked for a lot of outside stimulation. *(laughter)* I've got more than I can handle just in this room, you know! *(laughter)* When I look at the first film, *A Documentary*, I have to admit that I haven't changed in more than ten years. I began with an obsession with death and the film I'm making now continues that obsession. The challenge? *(pause)* Filmmaking has lost its challenge for me now, because over the years I've started caring more about life than film. For most serious filmmakers, film is more important than life to them.

GN: When you got out of school did you ever try working professionally — in television, for instance?

FC: My obsession with death wouldn't allow it. I think I've been saying life is too short all my life. Mom and Dad told me the other day that when I was a little kid I said I didn't have enough time. Nothing's changed. *(chuckle)*

GN: When you decided to make a film in Algeria, the logistics of putting that together were incredible. Why was it called *A Death* originally?

FC: *(long pause)* Can I answer that at the end? *(laughter)*

GN: But why did it become *A Life*?

FC: I changed. *(pause)* Okay, I'll answer that now. It's an autobiographical film. The reason I made the film was to decide what to do with my life. It was called *A Death* because while making the film I decided that the way I wanted to die was by suicide. I was so against death that this was the only way I saw of being able to beat it, meaning it won't kill me. I'm the one who's going to do it. Have I explained that?

GN: Yes, at the time your friends, including me and people like Tiff Findley, were very worried because we knew it was on your mind. You didn't talk about it but we knew by the bleakness of your life at the time that you were contemplating it. We knew it was the kind of thing you'd do. You were isolating yourself too quickly; everybody was concerned.

FC: But you have to understand that I wasn't planning to commit suicide at thirty. The plan was to commit suicide when I got old.

GN: It's explained very well in the film, because it's so minimal. The starkness of a single room whose only other complement is the desert. Did you know that at the time?

FC: I was just trying to get my life down on film, the life I wanted to lead. You can see how that obviously led to crossing the Sahara. The hardest thing about making the film was that I changed in the middle of it, which is why the title changed from *A Death* to *A Life*. I found out about life extension, which is a new branch of science that fights against aging. So suicide became unnecessary.

GN: You use two scenes from your first film that are very effective. I refer to them as the guillotine scenes. It feels that you're completing something, that experience is being abruptly chopped away with the death of your grandmother.

FC: I think it's perceptive that you picked up on that scene because it's the only one in the film that doesn't belong. Originally it opened the film. I'll explain it in a clearer way. *(pause)* I put that scene in the film as a rehearsal of my own suicide. I tried to separate it from the rest of the film by placing it before the titles. The first couple of times it was shown like that, but now it's in the body of the film.

GN: The other scene that was really involving is the destitute car scene in the desert with the guy crawling around. It feels like the end of something. Is that what you wanted there?

FC: I hoped that scene would symbolize ... *(long pause)* a rejection of death. The character really puts himself in the middle of shit by doing that.

GN: I interpret it as: what's the point?

FC: I meant exactly the opposite. This is it. Now he's got to walk his way out of it. I think the film is flawed by not explaining itself well enough. It's hard to understand.

GN: Did you have a sense of satisfaction when the film was done?

FC: I felt I could finally get on with my life instead of wasting it making a film.

GN: What's it like to sit in an audience of 400 people and watch your personal statements?

FC: *(long pause)* I don't think it has any effect on me. I value people's opinions but I don't want to change the film. *(pause)* What I should have said is that it doesn't bother me to be known intimately by audiences. Look at what I'm saying to you, Gary. *(robust laughter)* I just told you that at thirty I planned to commit suicide.

GN: Yes, but everybody knew that, Frank. They called you Mr. Doomsday. It wasn't a secret.

FC: They called me Dr. Death. *(chuckles)*

GN: What do you think of money? It's got nothing to do with making a film when it's only an idea, or when you're shooting, but it makes everything possible.

FC: I'm the type of person who doesn't think much about money. I think it is possible to make a film for less than is usually spent. I'm lucky because the type of films I'm making can be done very cheaply. I was given $50,000 to make *A Life*.

GN: Frank, for the average working stiff, that's his life's savings. *(laughter)* What was the first clue that you were not finished with filmmaking?

FC: Discovering life extension. It's possible to beat death, or at least to delay aging.

GN: So you get 120 years instead of 100. Does that count?

FC: It's a big difference to me. I wanted others to believe in life extension, too, because if we want to find out how to delay aging we have to spend money on it. That's what the new film is about. I wanted to prove that nothing is impossible. That's the message of the film, because through life extension, aging and death can be beaten. Most people didn't really understand what was involved in it. I think the main thing that helped get the money to cross the Sahara was

that I did a short training run, which gave me credibility. I went in 1988 and travelled 400 kilometres with a guide and a camel. It was an introduction to what I expected from the Saharans, and that's what I got. People all across the Sahara treated me like family, like a son. Absolutely like a son. *(chuckle)* It's tough coming back here after that. *(laughter)* I mean in this room — there's no affection here. *(robust laughter)*

GN: Is the desert forgiving?

FC: I found out how violent the desert is. By the last third of the trip I was living in fear most of the time because of the unexpected. The amount of things that can go wrong boggle the mind. By the time I got to the last country, Sudan, I thought I'd seen everything. I thought it would be a piece of cake the rest of the way, and it was the hardest country. Even in the last sixty kilometres things occurred that had never happened before. My camel was stolen while I was sleeping, so I had to walk the last sixty kilometres. The story of the crossing is full of problems. But that was why I went, it was my choice.

GN: Do you miss it?

FC: Yes. Terribly. Life is more of a pleasure in the Sahara than here.

GN: Do the people who live there know that?

FC: No. I think they have the same attitude toward life that we have here. It's a lot harder, but they don't know anything else, so they're used to it.

GN: It must have been odd for them to come across a man strolling across the desert in his black jeans and T-shirt.

FC: There were many times when I felt extreme grati- tude or when I was happier to see people than I've ever been. But in general, unfor- tunately, I had to avoid as much contact with people as possible because it was too tiring. I avoided spend- ing nights with people because it meant they'd want to talk to me. I was always so tired at the end of every day that I'd eat and go to sleep as quickly as possi- ble. Apart from the loneliness, the most difficult thing about crossing was fatigue. I had to be extremely conscious of conserving energy.

GN: How far was it?

FC: Seven thousand kilometres from the Atlantic Ocean to the Red Sea. In the summer it was 108 in the shade every day, 20 degrees hotter in the sun. It took eleven months, less about a month and a half when I was delayed.

GN: What's it like to put a foot in loose sand?

FC: It's more difficult to walk across. There's a myth that people travel across dunes by camel. They don't. They go around them because camels have a lot of trouble walking through sand dunes.

GN: What's a camel like?

FC: Gentle animal. But it's not domesticated like a dog. Camels are companions. They don't like being touched or ridden. They howl every time you load them. To think that they can not only walk those distances across the Sahara but carry huge weights, plus a person. For me to walk one day in the Sahara without carrying anything would exhaust me by lunch. I admire camels a lot. It took eight to cross. Most of the time I travelled with two at a time because I had to

carry enough water. The extra camel carried baggage and water. A couple collapsed from exhaustion. One of them fainted. One of them dropped to its knees and couldn't get up again. Another walked until it came to a stop. Those are the signs of complete exhaustion. I was able to ride two of them. The other one I pulled.

GN: What did you do when they collapsed?

FC: I waited until the next day and they regained enough strength to be able to get to the next village, where I could replace them.

GN: Did you have any water for them?

FC: No, I could never spare water for them. But it's normal for them to go a few days without water. Even with two camels, I could carry only three days of water. The problem is, when travelling by compass, one degree can put you out by sixty miles. In most cases wells are found by spotting people or animals. Who knows how many wells I rode by without even seeing them? There were many cases where I accidentally ran into a well that I couldn't have seen from 100 metres away. I remember one afternoon I became too sick to stand, so I had to stop and wait. I found out the next day by accident that I was a stone's throw from a well. It makes you feel good to find people because it means you're safe. People are safety. But it also makes you a little afraid. The more I got to know the Sahara, the more afraid I became. How are you going to see a hole in the ground?

GN: Are the Bedouins great navigators?

FC: Yes, all of the Saharans are. One night while I was sleeping, one of my camels was stolen. Fortunately, I happened to be a couple of kilometres away from a village that had police. I walked there and told them what happened and they immediately put me in a jeep and started tracking it. *(chuckle)* You wouldn't believe how they could do it, tracking a footprint in the Sahara. *(laughter)* They found it that evening.

GN: What happened to the thief?

FC: He was camped for the night, and when he saw the lights of the jeep coming he took off. Fortunately the police didn't try to chase him. I was worried that they might shoot him. They had their guns out, and life is cheap there. The penalty for camel theft is being shot and, you know, you would have to accept it.

GN: Did you think about moving at night rather than the daytime?

FC: I would have got lost. Only a percentage of the trip was guided by compass and a lot of it was by road, by camel path and some by guide. Though even when you're on a vehicle path you're always using the compass because there are no signs and you can't be sure of where the paths are really going. I had to force myself to take pictures every time. I did most of the filming in the morning before I started out, to conserve energy, before loading and unloading, which is tiring. The rest was done by carrying the tripod and camera outside of my baggage so I could get at it any time. I brought two Bolexes, spring-loaded and hand-cranked with 100-foot loads. I had three prime lenses: normal, wide-angle and a long lens. A friend of mine made a timer. So I set it for whenever I wanted it to start the camera shooting me.

I needed a camera that could hold up against the sand. If this was the Sahara and we opened that window, after a day you'd have a fine layer of sand over everything. It's very heavy dust and always in the air. I couldn't film during sandstorms; that was a sure way of losing the camera. I tried once with my stills camera and it jammed and I couldn't get it fixed. In the capital of Chad, an English guy lent me a stills camera to finish the trip with. I shot 4,500 feet of motion-picture film. Because of the fatigue of shooting and travelling, I had to make every shot count. I didn't have the strength to do anything extra. I took a lot more originally and sent it back. I had 7,000 feet at the beginning. I'd planned to send what I'd filmed back when I got halfway across and have some-one look at it and send a letter so I could find out if there were problems. Shortly after beginning the trip, I had an opportunity to send film back with someone who was going to Montreal. The main question was: am I getting heat damage or scratching?

GN: How did it happen that you ran into someone going back to Canada?

FC: When I was arrested and brought to the capital, I was there for a month. I met a guy whose mother lives in Canada. He was from an island off the coast of Africa and they were both going to be there in the future. He gave the film to her and she brought it back to Montreal.

GN: What did the guides think of you?

FC: We didn't like each other and got into a lot of fights. They didn't know what I was doing and I couldn't tell them how far I was really going. But the problems were all about them trying to cheat me in one way or another. My thinking from the beginning was that I should only travel with a guide when I thought it was impossible for me to find wells alone. But when I go back to do the next trip I'll do everything I can not to travel with guides again.

GN: What's the water of the desert like?

FC: Terrible. Well, when I say terrible I'm looking at it from your point of view. For me it was the greatest pleasure of my life. First of all, the water was almost always muddy. Water can be cooled by carrying it in animal skins. The constant evaporation causes cooling. The disadvantage of animal skins is that the water doesn't last as long, and the skin sheds and leaches colour, so the water is a little dirtier. I was also carrying water in plastic jerry cans.

GN: What did you do for sound on your trip?

FC: I recorded nothing. When I did the training run, I recorded everything I thought I'd need. Wind or silence.

GN: Are the people on the Atlantic different than people on the Red Sea?

FC: The common denominator was hospitality. They would have done anything for me.

GN: Do you think they respected you for doing it? Someone must have asked what you were doing out there.

FC: Unfortunately, I had to hide what I was doing because there was always the risk I would be picked up as a spy. If I told someone I was riding 7,000 kilometres across the desert, the Saharan way of thinking would be that only a government could get behind a project like that. I was arrested as a spy in Chad. They didn't even ask any questions, they just grabbed me. It was the biggest scare of the trip. They caught me as I was camping for the night, and as usual, I was so exhausted that I wasn't thinking straight enough to say anything about who I was and where I'd come from. Five men stood in a circle holding guns while others searched my baggage and I believed there was a fifty-fifty chance they would execute me. The strangest thing was that I wasn't scared but I was extremely sad. I was too tired to be scared. They took me to the next village and put me in jail. The next day they drove me to the capital a few hundred kilometres away and I was questioned by the police. They realized I wasn't a spy and I was allowed to go free.

GN: What convinced them that you were just a crazy tourist?

FC: They took everything I had, so they went through all my baggage and papers. I had reference letters from the Canada Council and the National Film Board explaining what I was doing. The next twenty-seven days were spent trying to get permission to keep going. Then I was stopped and delayed twice more across Chad and had to go through the same thing. The problem is that Chad was fighting rebels who have since taken over. Everybody was afraid to take responsibility for my safety, because my route went through the fighting. A lot of strange things happened on that trip because of the hardships and difficult conditions, but all in all, I want to go back. *(laughter)* You want to sublet this place, Gary? Your turn! You can have a turn in here now! *(robust laughter)* I'll be waiting for you halfway across there. You know, somebody asked me the other day when I was going to start dating women again. Then he said, "I guess I understand. The type of woman you're looking for would be someone you met halfway across the Sahara. Going the other way." *(chuckles)*

GN: Are you impressed that in Canada there exists an organization like the Canada Council that would actually give you money?

FC: My feeling is gratitude for all the help I've received over the years. Unfortunately, I think I've let people down over the years.

GN: Why?

FC: I've never become famous and I don't think I ever will. Why do you think they've helped me this much? Have they helped me more than anybody else?

GN: The unique thing about your work is how personal it is. It's very unusual that there is somebody with the vision to understand the artistry of your life and say, "Let's give this guy $30,000 and see if he dies." *(hearty laughter)* But that's what they're doing.

FC: You think so?

GN: Well, you might not have made it. How are they going to collect? You were a trigger away from not being here and nobody would have known. Where's Frank?

FC: Yes, that's true. Many times no one would have ever traced me. But people have done things that are a lot more dangerous. I've never gone to war.

GN: Is this your last movie?

FC: *(chuckle)* No, but I think it's the last for years, because I want to go to medical school and become a doctor. That won't allow me to make a film for years. The hardest thing about making this film is that there were many situations where I couldn't film for different reasons. For example, I couldn't film when I was arrested. Or when I was lost for a while or couldn't find a well. The first thing I had to do was get out of trouble. There was no time to waste filming. It's too bad. I've learned that there was something I wasn't strong enough to cope with. All my life I found that just by forcing myself to do something I was always able, out of sheer willpower. But I found in the Sahara that there existed something that I wasn't strong enough to cope with. And that was loneliness. Specifically loneliness for people who are dead. I thought about it while riding and dreamed about it at night. The pain was more than I could cope with. I had to block it out.

GN: Was that stronger than the physical pain?

FC: For me it was. No comparison. Thirst was the only thing that came close. Thirst was the second-biggest pain in the Sahara. But it was a double-edged sword because it was also what gave me the biggest pleasure. I was so thirsty every time I drank that I found myself either thinking or saying out loud that this is all I need. I absolutely meant it, Gary. I didn't need marriage, children, house, work, sex, money, nothing. Water was enough for me, it completely filled my life. That's hard for people to understand. *(robust laughter)* But you can get so thirsty, that's what water means to you. Several times a day you're in a situation where you've got to drink or you're going to die, or you're going to start dying. Thirst has reached the point where you're going to start weakening and then you're going to get sick, and then you're going to die. You know, maybe you are a day away from death. *(chuckle)* You're thirsty. *(laughter)*

Correspondences

To Live or Not to Live
Peter Mettler

My earliest memory of Frank is when he told me about writing the script for his first feature, *A Life*. He worked in a room that contained only a desk and several sheets of Letraset (a pre-computer technology that offered sheets filled with alphabets that could be rubbed onto a page one letter at a time). I imagine this meticulous, well-trimmed man, dressed in black in a white room, rubbing the words of his ideas onto paper as they became clear in his mind, single letter by single letter. It is likely he already knew his ideas inside and out, having repeated them to himself over and over like a mantra before committing them to paper. The act of scriptwriting was probably more like ritual devotion for Frank, in itself a work of art.

Though it is hard to say what Frank might have considered Art. He was not a typical, or even typically atypical, artist, dedicated neither to self-expression, exploring the unknown or saving the world. For me, Frank was a completely enigmatic and charmingly obsessive individual whom I admired greatly for always getting back to the point. His life was largely dedicated to a prolonged attention to detail, exploring the very essence of what it means to stay alive.

Frank thrived on the line between death and life. He had a profound fear of, and fascination with, death that, from an outside perspective, occupied his every move and motive and movie. As an audience, we can first see this in the portrait of his grandmother's death in *A Documentary*. I remember being quite moved when I first saw this film, together with his Ottawa Valley hillbilly portrait, *The Mountenays*. Both looked at real life with a loving, poignant intensity. My subsequent first visit with Frank was at his home, where he lived at the time with his parents, and all seemed exceptionally normal. What I didn't realize until meeting him in person was the utter horror he felt about his grandpa's death. His grandfather died a normal death of old age. What I had seen in Frank's film was a beautiful engagement with a loved one's passing, but for Frank, the unacceptable injustice of death contravened the beauty and power of life itself. I recall the earnest emotion in his voice when he contemplated life's ending, whether his or anyone else's. He would begin to quiver as if he had a gun to his head right then and there. It simply seemed wrong to him, like a flaw in the master plan, and he was intent on doing everything in his power to get around it.

Both Frank and I would be turning fifty around now, so it has been a while since our early encounters, which occurred nearly twenty years ago. Some recollections are hazy while others have gained a nearly mythic dimension. Frank's presence lent a larger-than-life quality to even casual encounters, like a discussion that occurred during a drive from Montreal to Ottawa, our last in-person meeting of any substantial length.

Frank had spent years preparing for his first solo Sahara crossing, a journey that became his last complete film. His preparations involved a lot of intense physical training as well as extensive survival studies. He had already shot one film in the desert that many feared he would not return from. Frank is pretty black-and-white about things, so at some point I asked him the most obvious question: Why was he doing this?

He explained that the best way to deal with his fear, to overcome the threat of death, is to push life to the very edge of itself. It is necessary to confront death with the will and defiance to live, and this is best done while enduring the most threatening circumstances.

I have never much feared death. Even as a teenager I was even quite curious about it, and still am. My very first Super 8 film, made when I was sixteen years old, was called *Reverie*, and shows death sold as a dream to an unsuspecting mortal by a guardian gypsy woman.

Accordingly, my answer to Frank's strategy was something like: Why don't you accept death as an inevitable part of life? Why not overcome your fear by embracing the realization that we are all part of something larger than ourselves? We only exist in coordination with everything around us, in an interdependent way…

But no, he insisted, death had to be surmounted. Even if it meant freezing his body so it could be reawakened in some unknown future, there must be a way to perpetuate life. Life against death was a battle that had to be fought as though they were opponents.

But, I retorted, maybe being dead is another aspect of living. Maybe you would actually be short-changing yourself to be forever living. Maybe life and death are not polarities, but one and the same!

Frank abhorred decay and transformation, disappearance, loss of control. It's compelling to see him as a kind of contemporary superhero, firmly lodged in the illusion of identity, whose mission is to defy both logic and death. It's interesting, too, that he chose nature as his challenger — the desert, the limits of his own body — while the thing that finally killed him was just another man.

I can't say I knew him well, but I loved talking with Frank because it always came to the same meaningful point — what are we doing here? There was no chit-chat except for a bit of technical talk. It made me wonder: did he laugh with glee while he surfed, or did he maintain the same earnestness that possessed him whenever we met? One night he took me to Hull — the wild side of Ottawa — to go dancing. He prefaced this excursion by saying that sometimes he really liked to let loose. Indeed, I saw the spectacle of Frank Cole on the dance floor — stiffly shifting weight from one leg to the other, symmetrically and systematically, not unlike his films.

None of my propositions about the acceptance of death ever added up for Frank. He would repeat his feelings about confronting death using different language shadings, and we would speak in circles. It's not really a conclusive kind of discussion — at least for the living.

We were all amazed and proud of Frank for having made the Sahara trek and a one-of-a-kind filmic document to accompany it. Editing seemed a longer trek than the journey itself! I saw a rough cut of the film, and then two years later the final version, which looked pretty much the same as the previous cut. It is hard to imagine either of those processes. I talked to Frank again on the phone during that time without reopening our discussion. He'd done it. He'd confronted death and won. So what was he going to do next? He was going to do it again! I believe we filmmakers make variations of the same film over and over again. But Frank was so succinct. He was on a loop.

Myths being what they are, the next chapter seemed both epic and inevitable. And so it was, at some desert outpost, that his body and a few exposed rolls of film were one day found to reveal the loss of Frank's life. For many who knew Frank the news did not come as a shock — but as a surprise nonetheless. It is the surprise we feel when impermanence insists once more, and someone you love and count on as part of life disappears.

We often want proof of those departed. Frank Cole's films are a documented trajectory of his own ultimate destination. The last black-and-white rolls of film he shot, perhaps only a day before his passing, contained images of burial grounds. Therein lie the remains of some who might have known the secret just before he did.

Frank Cole
305 Gloucester St. Apt. 5
Ottawa
Canada K1R 5E3

DEAD
NAKED.

RICK TAYLOR
819 LYON ST. S.
APT. 3
OTTAWA, ONT.

Guayaquil, Ecuador.

It is October 13.

I am in Political
Trouble, here.

Rick Taylor
819 Lyon St. S.
Apt. #3
Ottawa,
Canada. K1S 9A2

REPUBLICA DEL ECUADOR
QUITEX'83
s/ 3=

QUITEX'83
s/ 3=
REPUBLICA DEL ECUADOR

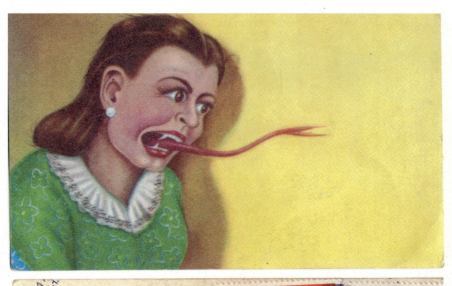

U.S. ARTIC.
12. 6. 99

I'M DRIVING 20,000 KMS.
BUT I WANT MUCH MORE.
FRANK.

USA 20

RICK TAYLOR
61 RUETER CRES.
NEPEAN, ONTARIO
CANADA.

DECEMBER 10.

POST CARD

RICK TAYLOR
"PROSPERO BOOKS"
BILLINGS BRIDGE PLAZA
RIVERSIDE DR.
OTTAWA, CANADA.

Air Mail   Par avion

tchad

tchad

MAO, Préfecture du KANEM.
A la fin des pluies, la ville construite à la limite
du désert sur la colline sableuse bordée de deux
«ouaddi» se transforme en oasis : eau, sable, soleil
et palmiers s'y marient dans la douce lumière
du soir.

© Photo BWASO - COLLECTIONS DIALOGUE DE CIVILISATIONS
Autorisations N° 195 et 273/MDPR/INFO/85 - Réf. 89/475

MAY 17, 90
N'DJAMENA

WAS PUT IN JAIL HERE
FOR 1 NIGHT. JUST EARLIER
I THOUGHT I MIGHT BE
EXECUTED. WHAT I FELT
WASN'T FEAR. IT WAS
SADNESS.

RICK TAYLOR
61 RUETER CRESCENT
NEPEAN, ONTARIO
CANADA

K2J 3Z9

FRANK COLE

April 15, 84
Ouargla.

"You would be happier if
you had no eyes", this
blind woman said.

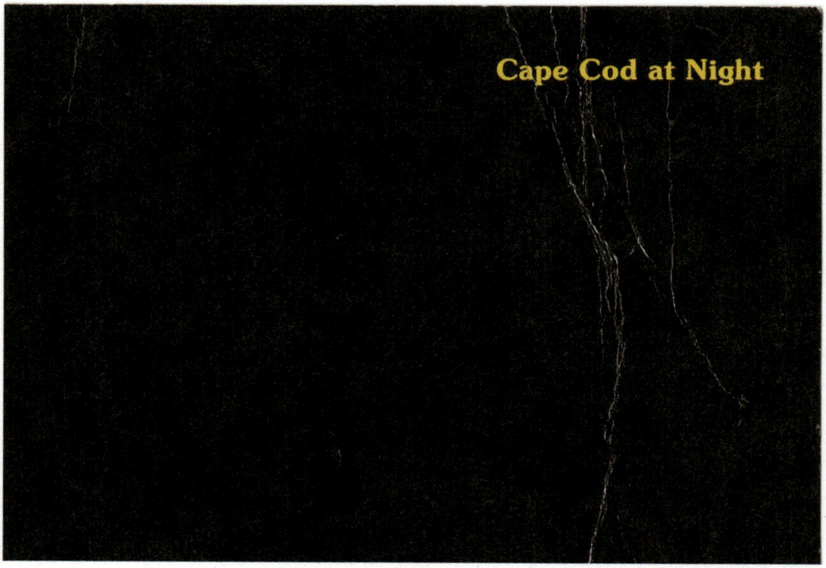

Cape Cod at Night

CAPE COD

25 USA

FRANK

POST CARD

RICK, DALE, SKY TAYLOR

819 LYON ST. S.

APT. 1

OTTAWA

CANADA

70 km from Timbuktu

Lisa Cole

Where the four directions meet, where all the images
converge, where your shadow rose to greet you:
this is where the lost film plays over and over.

In a frozen still, the light burns around
you. The light erases your features, cuts you
out of the picture. You're a black hole,
surrounded by light. We see your outline,
sharp as the Earth's edge.

You and your famous black hat.

                    ***

Someone took scissors to the body of
your work. We collect your pieces, kneel on the
cutting room floor, trying to splice the
story back together. But you're twisting on
your own now, reanimating.
Fragments of celluloid coalesce into
random sequences, endless permutations of
your life and death and all the
possibilities in between.

My art is my blueprint for life.

                    ***

You gave us a detailed map, so we
could keep track of you. We marked the
places as you passed through:
Rabat, Atar, Tidjikdja,
Timbuktu …

Moving myself 25 km per day takes so much strength
that I have nothing left for letters, for anything.

Karachi, 1963. You're a nine-year-old savage,
already grinning from the back of a camel.
Political turmoil. The Embassy is
sending wives and children home to
Canada; but your father must remain.
You dig a trench in the backyard for
him to hide in. Already, fear of
death is not a stranger.

Nomads follow the rain.

***

Genetic memory calls you back to
Africa. Voices of loved ones buzz, trying to
dissuade you. The Sahara has an
overwhelming gravity, pulling eyes
from their sockets, planes from the
sky.

I've been trapped by the Sahara summer.

You carry your grandfather on your
shoulders. You find well after well, cracked and
dry. The worst drought in years,
they say.

It was the most difficult Sahara I've ever done.
There was a point where I did not see a person for
eight days.

70 km southeast of Timbuktu. The light is
perfect here. You stop to wind the timer on your
Bolex. If you're quick, you'll catch your
shadow in the sunset.

Come and get me motherfuckerdeath.
This is what it means.

You are fully absorbed. It seems like you've
waited your whole life for this one moment in
time that goes on and on now, forever —
captured on film by invisible cameras,
projected by haunted imaginations. You
do not hear bandits approaching.

You stare them straight in the eye.

Getting lost over and over is like Russian roulette.
It must always end in death.

We see you sitting in the sand with your footprints
all around you. A great wind comes along,
vanishing them.

Sahara seems endless. I long for life
to be endless, too.

Now you are walking away from the
camera, dissolving into the
sand, the wind, the relentless glare
of our projectors.

70 km from a place that doesn't exist
with your focus ring set on
infinity.

Reading the Desert
Deirdre Logue

A Death Made

Watching Frank's films, which open and close with his grandfather's last moments, made me think of my own endings. Frail and oblivious, I am hoping my fall from grace will be short and painless. Knowing it will be so much more besides, I struggle to absorb Frank's stark images. It takes a while to adjust to the light, but once inside his proposition, Frank proves an irresistible draw: his films are a magnetic field that surrounds us both.

Less isn't more in Frank's films, less is less, and we don't get much of that either. Frank's films document the taking away of so much — the telephone, the cabinet, the lamp, a breath — all stolen away from the lens in an urgent, almost mean kind of way, as if we've had a fight. Frank begins by taking away everything he doesn't need, which, as it turns out, is almost everything.

After these removals, the scene is set and Frank moves with precision into preparation, action and reflection. The framework is so simple, so spare at times, that the sound of his voice arrives as a shocking intrusion. Frank's self-portraits are carefully organized; nothing is approximate or taken for granted. We see Frank as he would wish us to see him: lean and focused. He is pure purpose.

Frank's films are a consideration of detail and always he begins with questions of form: the composition, the shape of the light, the picture plane revealed. What he is busy recording is not the place where he is, or his journey, or his hopes. He is recording instead the place these might have rested, once, when he was still human. The pictures of his grandfather do not show death at work, instead, they are death itself, the raw embodied experience, endured again and again in an endless walk across the desert.

Frank Like Me

I do not wonder who is taking these pictures of Frank because even though I know there has to be someone else, these pictures are by Frank and Frank alone. His room, where he trains for his walks, is like a desert in miniature: flat, dry, barren, hard, full of snakes and rage. Teeming with potential thieves, this place is a temporary map. Like me, Frank starts only what he knows he can finish. He chooses small spaces at first to test his abilities. He overprepares, turns the camera toward his efforts and takes his last steps for the first time.

Once the room is clear, it is time for the larger room of the desert. The clearing never stops. What he is showing us, frame after frame, is the act of clearing the room. For the sake of his invisible pictures, Frank's teenage defiance is quickly overcome by barren stretches of land. Fanning from his tired shoulders, the desert becomes wings. The longer he walks, the older the young Frank gets, and like me, Frank gets better-looking. His aging accelerates as he gets closer to what he wants. Frank is becoming familiar with this place, we see him as part of it now, realizing he will not be turning back. Like me, Frank prefers ground to sky, and likes to pretend he needs no one. Driven by the impossible, Frank tends toward the immersive.

As Frank walks, the serpent rises. He drinks the dead man's water and skins a snake on principle. Frank asks the scorpion to give in, just this once, for him. His beard grows slowly to better outline his face. What looks like water turns out to be gasoline, while air becomes fire. Bathing in a mirage of soap, Frank stays clean. And swallows, loudly.

The Learning Curve

Watching his films, I learn that deserts may not receive more than ten inches of rain per year. Deserts are often covered with rocks and pebbles and surfaces much less glamorous than those silken mountains of fine red sand reproduced in airline magazines. I learn that deserts aren't so much about what they have, but about what they don't have. Deserts are cold at night because they lack cloud cover to retain the day's warmth. What kills most often isn't heat or thirst, but lack of food.

Some deserts don't see rain for fifty years, though fog may bring reprieve. It arrives overnight and leaves a magnificent dew, dripping from sharp needles. Droplets touch down on seeds, some of which have lain in a dormant state for thirty years, waiting for this very day when just enough moisture will arrive to waken them. At night, bats drink from short-lived cactus flowers. In the morning, desert locusts emerge just as small plants bloom for the first and last time.

Watching Frank's films, my romantic attachment to the desert wanes and I can better regard the menace, the crust. The Sahara looks like Africa's necklace and Frank follows along the throat. Entire days slip past as he attempts to record his picture. He labours, fighting panic. I learn to keep going.

Sky's the Limit

Lately I have felt tearful, thin-skinned, paranoid and distrustful. Events accumulate on my surface. It's very different from the horizonless horizon of the desert, where the optic nerve is released in a succession of panoramas. As I return from a trip to London, my eyes are still turned inward, recoiling from the

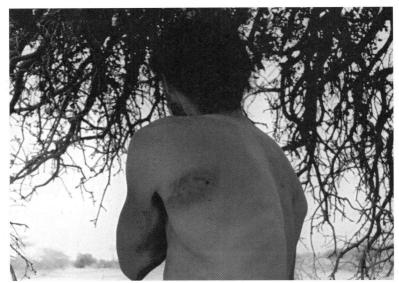

congestion and surveillance cams. My flight from Heathrow to Toronto is still in progress while I write this. The sky outside my face-shaped window is 39,000 feet above the soil and concrete and ocean below, yet it looks a lot like its desert cousin, sharing a beautiful strangeness. Lacking the warmth of the desert but having many of its other characteristics, the sky is inhospitable, vast and unrepeatable.

I have been up in the sky many times without ever once hoping for it. Instead, I have always wanted to go to the desert, but managed only once. My parents used to vacation in the Arizona roadside, and it was there we took our last trip as a family. We were soon torn apart with confusion as my dad, unbeknownst to us, suffered from dementia. At night he would wake me up over and over again to help him find the car keys. Each day as the sun blazed onto the golf course just outside, my dad stayed indoors and watched the Weather Channel with great concentration, his hand trembling as it hovered over the remote to prevent unwanted channel change.

On a more recent trip to Arizona, I travel without my dad (and from then on it is the same; this trip marks a new moment of decline — when we greet each other we are also leaving, we are both alone in a new way). My girlfriend, mother and I drive for three hours around the Apache Trial. Terribly carsick, I cling to the passenger door and notice signs that seem to guide or point us forward. I take pictures with a small disposable camera purchased at the last place we saw people. Back home, the pictures show the difference between signs pointing in the right direction and signs pointing in the only direction.

On the flight I watch the film *Juno*. Like the lead character, my sister is also pregnant, and I hope my dad will feel ready to go after the baby is born. He knows nothing about her baby, which is due close to his birthday on September 10, seventy-six years ago. The beginning of one life and the end of another. Will my sister's child make it easier for me to say the last words as if they were enough?

My dad keeps fighting. Caught between living yes and no. Why won't he give up and give in, release himself and all of us from this terrible stasis? I want his death to come sooner than later, and in this wish there is also the beginnings of writing, and an inevitable delay. I watch the films again and see Frank's grandfather about to die. Ready or not, he is moments away and I know I have to write about this too. Most often when I look, I can see Frank walking again, facing death, pushing past his fears. The writing is not a way to speak about my father or about Frank Cole, but a suggestion, a whisper, of how one might approach what cannot be said.

The plane still in the air, I see the sky, clouds underneath us now like the coarse salt on the desert floor that willingly takes the shape of Frank's boots. How much longer?

Sahara Journal
Frank Cole

Introduction

The reason why I crossed the Sahara desert by camel had to be kept a secret. I will explain why, later. The Sahara desert is 7,000 kilometres wide and took eleven months to cross. I was thirty-six: young, extremely fit, extremely determined. For now I am only going to explain that I did it to prove something. I could prove it symbolically, not scientifically, because I am an artist, not a doctor. But I believe that symbolic proof might inspire others to discover scientific proof. Nothing is impossible.

November 29, 1989

I start across the Sahara. This is the moment for which I have made preparations on and off for four years. The moment I waited eight years for. The moment I have come to realize I gave up too much of life for. The moment is an ecstasy. A relief from pain. For a while.

My lost baggage and film equipment arrived November 18. My planned route is to take as straight a line as possible between the Sahara's approximate widest points: Nouakchott on the Atlantic Ocean to Suakin on the Red Sea. My first destination is a town called Magta Lahjar, 350 kilometres away. Because there is a road on my route, I am going to follow it except when it no longer runs straight.

A friend I have made here, Mohammed Cheigeur, is riding with me for two days to teach me enough about camel loading to continue on alone. As we ride parallel to the road through Nouakchott's outskirts, I notice soldiers come out of a building in the distance. In a few moments I realize they are heading to cut us off. They stop and wait for us to arrive.

"You aren't allowed here," one of the soldiers orders us. "This is a military zone."

We leave them and start to circle around the area. A few minutes later, I notice a soldier running desperately after us. Cheigeur does not notice. I point to the running soldier and tell Cheigeur to stop. The soldier is in a hurry to reach us. He sinks in the soft sand and tries to run faster. I wonder why he is tiring himself out in this heat? He reaches us out of breath. "The commander says he'll shoot unless you go back to the road immediately." We obey.

December 1, 1989

Cheigeur and I wave goodbye. I start the slow trot of a camel. It is mid-afternoon. I could not ride this morning because I had filming to do. I am holding my breath that my camel's load does not slip off. Two days ago, when I looked at the 200 pounds of baggage, it seemed overwhelming. I did not know how to tie a knot, except for the one in my shoelaces! I told myself to force myself through this. Though Cheigeur taught me the basics, I find it complicated. I also realize that if I can't learn to load as well as a Saharan, I will not make it across the Sahara. Loading is too tiring in this heat to have to repeat. Cheigeur had problems himself with my load. He had to stop to fix it eight times. I ride beside the road up the first dune. As I start down the other side, my saddle begins to tip forward more and more. By the time I get to the bottom of the dune, my saddle is tipped so far I am going to fall out. I stop and unload everything. I retie the saddle as tight as possible. I load again. Forty-five minutes later I start once more. There is another dune a short distance ahead; by the time I ride over it my saddle has tipped over again. I stop and camp early. There is no point in loading again, because it would be almost dark by the time I finished. I have ridden three kilometres today. I have 7,000 to go.

December 2

Loading takes an hour and a half this morning. By the time I finish, I am hot and drink quite desperately. I know that with experience I will learn to speed up. I know I have to. I will not be able to sustain the daily effort of loading in the morning, partial loading and reloading to rest the camel at lunch, and unloading at night. I ride against the wind that has come up. The wind drowns out all sound, that of my camel's footsteps and sloshing water supply, and becomes the only sound in the desert. I have not gone far when I notice a muffled thump. I turn around and see one of my water containers on the sand. Had the wind been any louder, I would not have heard it. I stop and reattach it, then continue. Soon my saddle is tipped too far forward to sit in. I get off and walk my camel. I come upon a few nomad tents, camouflaged until I get close enough to see through the haze of blowing sand. Though I have only done five kilometres this morning, I decide to stop early for lunch, to take advantage of being able to get help fixing my saddle. There is almost no traffic on this road: an average of five vehicles per day. Had the tents not been beside the road, I would have missed them in the blowing sand. I ask if I can rest inside until the midday heat is over. An old man comes out and helps me unload down to the saddle.

I am a little worried about how tired I am after only five kilometres. I lie down once I finish the tea and bowl of bread soaked in oil and sugar that his family kindly gives me. I am too tired to be kept awake by the sand blowing over my face through the entrance.

Forty minutes later, I get up and ask for a drink of water before I leave. A new woman who has arrived makes a praying gesture to me, meaning, am I a Muslim? So that I don't appear ungrateful for their hospitality by saying I am an atheist, I lie and tell her I am a Christian. In other words, we both believe in the same God. Nevertheless, she makes an angry gesture to the old man which tells him that he should refuse me a drink. I am stunned. The Saharans are the most hospitable people in the world. I look at the old man. He looks scared and hesitates, then tells his son to give me a drink. When I finish, I reach out my hand to the old man to thank him and say goodbye. He trembles slightly, and hesitates again. I wave goodbye. I do not ask for help fixing my saddle. I know they would not. Fortunately, a man from one of the other tents sees me, reties my saddle and helps me reload. But to be sure my saddle does not tip over again today, I walk on foot for the rest of the afternoon.

December 3
A few men from a village I stayed at last night help me load this morning. I leave but come back two minutes later. My saddle is already tipping. They help me unload and we start again. Then I ride the rest of the morning without a problem. Seventeen kilometres — as much as I did in the last two days together! My excitement does not last long. In the late afternoon the saddle tips, and I am walking again. At dinner I realize the walking was more of an effort than I thought. I drink seven mugs of water. Just before I get into my sleeping bag, to be sure I can get to sleep, I drink one more. This is the beginning of winter, and temperatures are only in the 90s Fahrenheit in the shade. How bad will thirst be in summer?

December 4
Heat and fatigue are synonyms. It is 92 degrees F in the shade. In the sun I estimate it is 15 degrees hotter. This is an estimate because I am only carrying an ordinary thermometer, one that measures temperature in the shade, not the sun. I am resting in the shade of a thorn tree. Resting at lunch, through the worst of the heat, is a compulsory routine of camel travel. For the camel too. I have unloaded mine down to the saddle, to rest him more while he grazes on the thorn trees and scrub. Because the saddle's weight is negligible to him, to conserve

energy I do not unload it. The first thing I have to do after unloading is drink immediately. The second thing, eat. I cook a bowl of rice and dates, and then another. The food soon has an adrenalin-like effect. Fatigue subsides. Thirst does not subside for long. I drink a few mugs of water and a few coffees. This morning I finished filming the first roll of my film about this trip. I realize already that I will have to do most of the filming in the mornings before riding, while I am still fresh. I am writing this book at lunch every day for the same reason. By night I am too tired to think straight. I bring my camel into the shade to reload. In spite of the shade, by the time I finish I have to drink again from my water skin. The single most important tool against the heat is the Saharan water skin, because it provides water that is cool. It does this by sweating water, which, as it evaporates, cools the water skin. Without the water skin, I would not be capable of attempting to cross the Sahara. Neither could I do without a hat and sunglasses. Without their shade, exhaustion would soon stop me. Sooner or later, though, exhaustion is inevitable. No tool or method can prevent fatigue, only reduce it as it accumulates. Exhaustion is the end result of accumulated fatigue.

December 5

By 10:30 a.m. I am loaded. By 11:30 a.m. my saddle is tipped too far to sit in. I have to stop. This time I do not know if I can ignore the saddle and walk, because it is now biting into his back, making him howl periodically in pain. It is already taking three hours a day loading and unloading. The thought of another hour and a half, now in the midday sun, makes me balk momentarily. I stand motionlessly beside my camel. I gather my strength together. A minute

goes by. I have an idea. I sit back on my camel, behind the saddle. He does not howl. It is uncomfortable but will get me through to lunch, when I have to unload anyhow.

I painfully realize something now. Tomorrow, at Boutilimit, when the road no longer runs straight, I will not be capable of leaving it to cross open desert for 175 kilometres. When I saw how camouflaged the huts were in the blowing sand the other day, I began to wonder whether I had the experience for open desert yet. In a sandstorm, I could miss a small village a few hundred metres away, causing me to run out of water. Now I know I do not have the experience. I can't even load yet. Leaving the road now would be suicidal. A death wish, not a wish for death's death.

December 7

I am claustrophobic again after waking up. With my camel's first step, it vanishes. Will it be back tomorrow? And every day? I do not stop for rest at lunch; I prefer to keep making progress since it is only in the high 80s in the shade, so it is not hot enough to be forced to stop. I eat dates for lunch while I ride. I stuffed padding under my saddle's front end, to try to prevent it from tipping forward. So far so good. I do not let my camel walk. I keep him at a slow trot all day. I cover five kilometres an hour. My saddle holds. I make by far my best progress to date. A 44-kilometre day. I think the worst of the loading is over. Depending on whether I have to stop for rest at lunch or not, and until I learn to speed up, I should only have to cope with two to three hours of loading per day.

December 8

Back in Canada, my best friend and writer Richard Taylor is going through some of the logistics of my trip with me. "Have you decided what type of book you're going to write?" he asks me.

I hesitate. "I've changed my mind," I tell him. "I've decided not to write one. It's going to take everything I've got, just to cross the Sahara. There won't be anything left in me to make the film, much less to write a book too. I don't even know how I'll make the film. I don't know how I'll do it. It scares me, Rick. It really scares me."

A few days later, Rick arrives grimly at my apartment.

"Frank, I've got to insist you change your decision about the book. Only a book can tell the whole story. No film ever can, two hours isn't long enough. Frank, I've got to insist that you admit this: if there's no book, there is no Sahara."

I hated to admit it. I hated to. But I had to. He was right. I still didn't know how I'd do it, but I told Rick I would.

8 a.m.

It is starting to get hot as I unpack my camera to film. I find out that my camera's self-timer is not working. I change the batteries, but it still does not work. I change the cable for a new one; next I change the trigger; neither make it work. I oil it; this does not work. I go back to the beginning and start again. I change one battery that I suddenly notice is in wrong. It works. It occurs to me that in Canada I would never have put a battery in wrong. I must be a little tired from the heat and claustrophobia.

My camel threatens to bite me as I film myself trying to attach his reins. I jump out of the way in time. A camel bite can break a bone. The camera runs out and I wind it up and try again. The self-timer sticks from the blowing sand and does not work. I clean it and try again. My camel swings his head angrily around and around, snarls, threatens to bite me, grazes my shoulder, vomits over me, but I finally get his reins on. It has taken two hours to make this one shot of my film. I load my camel for the next hour and a half, knowing that by the time I have to stop riding to rest at lunch, I will have to force myself through fatigue to write my book.

December 9

I leave the road. I am capable of it now, because it is only 30 kilometres until I meet it again where it straightens out once more. It is the first experience riding by compass. When I camp for the night I have not reached the road, but I know I must be close. After dark I notice a tiny moving light in the distance. My camel strays farther and farther away from my camp as he grazes and looks for more food. When his shadow finally disappears into the darkness, I leave to find him. If I do not tie him up every night he could easily stray so far by morning that I would not be able to find him. I walk in the direction I saw him last. Two minutes later I see his shadow ahead. I have to give him until the last possible moment to graze. I make a mental note of the direction so I can find him when I'm ready to sleep, then turn around to go back to my camp. Clouds suddenly cover the moon, which is like turning off the only light in a room at night. I walk for a few minutes, then stop in my tracks. I have just realized I am lost and I am in trouble. Winter nights are so cold I have to sleep in a down sleeping bag with all my clothes on. It will be agony overnight if I do not find my camp. I stand still and listen. When I hear my camel's chewing, I re-orientate myself from where I am, then keep walking, but do not find it. I listen for his chewing again, walk back to re-orientate myself from where he is, but still do not find it. I know that my camp is only 75 metres away from my camel, but without moonlight it is as if it were 75 kilometres away. I crisscross in different directions, careful not to get out of earshot of his chewing. I notice something shiny a short distance away. I wonder what it is and walk up to it. My white jerry can.

December 10

I resume following the road, and stop for water at a village called Choggar, late in the afternoon. A man drawing water from a well for his donkey draws water for my camel. But when I start untying my water skin to fill it next, he gestures to me not to. "I'll take you to another well for that," he says. "This water is good for animals but not for people." I realize he means this well is contaminated with animal shit. He takes me to another nearby well. It is typical Saharan water, just like the other was: a dirty, light brown. This well is as likely to be contaminated as the other, because like the other well, it doesn't have a raised rim around it to keep out contamination. Water disinfection is impossible most of the time for me. Though I use a filter for a small amount of my water, it would be too exhausting to filter the staggering amount of water I need over the course of this trip. Boiling would be too exhausting. And in my opinion, chemical disinfection would be dangerous because of the high chemical exposure inherent in any high water consumption like mine. I fill my water skin, then fill my jerry can. If you are thirsty enough, you will drink anything. This is always the case here. Neither is there any point waiting until the next well for better water. The water will be

the same ahead, or sometimes worse. I will be sick many times before the end of this trip.

December 11

My camel is gone. It is morning, and I did not tie him up overnight, so he could graze better. I thought that because I had camped in Choggar it would be impossible for him to stray away unnoticed. But nobody has seen him. I ask an old man for help. He tells me to show him my camel's footprints. I take him to where I last saw my camel, just before dark. But the wind has blown across his footprints overnight. The old man searches the surrounding area for a trace. In the distance he finds the footprints of a hobbled camel. I had hobbled mine, tying his front ankles together to restrict his straying to a shuffle. He follows the footprints. It must be him. Suddenly a man's footprints enter, then both footprints continue together. Wrong camel.

The old man asks a shepherd tending goats who we run into if he has seen a camel. Then he asks two men on foot going to Choggar. Then a family at a hut on the village's outskirts. But nobody has seen him. The old man stops at a small reservoir to ask one more time. Nomads come to the reservoir from all directions, so if nobody here has seen him, I will never find him. A young man is watering a small herd of camels. We have walked a few kilometres to sit down on the sand to rest in some shade. A couple of the camels are pissing into the reservoir while they drink. The old man is thirsty and goes over and has a drink. I do not, though I need some water. The young man sits down with us. The old

man tells him, pointing to me: "He's looking for his camel. Did you see one on your way here?"

The young man draws a brand in the sand for me: X. "That's my camel," I say excitedly. "Where is he?"

"I'll take you there," he says, pointing west. "Your camel is quite far away." I realize something. There is plenty of grazing right here, therefore my camel has not strayed, looking for grazing. He has run away.

The young man collects his camels to take back to his tent. It is almost midday and hot to be walking, even at the leisurely pace of a camel herd. Three kilometres later, the young man points into the distance. At first, I do not see anything. Then I spot him: a small figure on account of the distance. As the old man and I approach, he takes a few desperate, hobbled jumps away from us. As the old man attaches his reins, the camel threatens to bite him. The old man jumps out of the way and falls down. Together we get his reins on. There is less grazing here than back at Choggar. Yes, he had run away.

We start the five-kilometre walk back to my camp. It is midday. The old man soon stops to catch his breath in some shade. I am glad for myself that he does. Dry spittle begins forming in my mouth. We step back out into the heat again. By the time we get back, the old man's face is pale with fatigue. I have to lie down. When I wake up, it is too late in the afternoon to start loading. No progress today. Not one kilometre.

December 13
No progress today, either: I have to spend all day filming. I am 20 kilometres past Choggar. The reason for filming all day is that I have to send some rolls back to Canada for developing on December 17 to check if I am having any technical problems before going too far with my film. Heat, for example, damages film permanently. Tomorrow when I arrive at Magta Lahjar, I will return to Nouakchott by vehicle to send them. I will make no progress for another week.

December 14
I arrive at my first destination: Magta Lahjar. This makes me think again about my progress. It is literally step by step across a continent. At this pace, my trip will come to seem endless. 360 kilometres down, 6,600 to go. I don't care about the distance. I must telephone my mother and father in Canada when I return to Nouakchott. I must know that nothing has happened to them.

December 15

The vehicle I am in makes the compulsory stop at the police checkpoint outside Nouakchott. A policeman points at me, ignoring the other passengers, who are Saharan.

"Get out," he orders. He takes me into his office. I am worried that if he finds my rolls of film, they will be confiscated because I do not have a Film Permit. I am making my film secretly, because the odds of Film Permit refusal are too high to risk the film being prohibited once it is known about. Mauritania is frightened about further media exposure of the immigrant massacres that took place recently. For a month and a half they considered refusing to allow me to come here on holiday.

"Give me your passport," he orders.

He sees I have a tourist visa.

"Why are you in Mauritania?"

"I'm a tourist," I answer politely.

He looks at me suspiciously. Foreigners do not come to Mauritania for tourism. Foreigners come to Mauritania only for work.

"Where are you going?"

"I'm going to Nouakchott, to say goodbye to a Canadian friend who's returning to Canada."

It is with my friend, Jean Chauvin, that I am sending the rolls back to Canada.

"Why is he in Mauritania?"

"He's the Canadian consul."

My name-dropping does not influence him.

"Where have you gone?"

"I went to Magta Lahjar by camel." Then to try name-dropping again, I add, "The police chief of Magta Lahjar is taking care of my camel until I return."

"What's your occupation?" he continues relentlessly.

"I'm an English teacher," I lie. That puts an end to any more questions into my occupation, at least. Nobody speaks English in Mauritania.

"Where are you staying in Nouakchott?"

"I'm staying at a friend's place."

"What's his name?"

"Tacha Fall."

He looks at me jealously. "Is she married?"

A Muslim woman with a Christian man is sacrilegious. We both know he has trapped me. Ironically, I have been celibate for more than four years.

Celibacy is one of the things I did to prepare myself to face this trip. But celibacy is unbelievable to a Saharan man.

"No, she is not married," I answer.

He thinks he has something on me now.

He searches my bag, finds my address book and opens it to Tacha's name. He looks at it for a long time. Then he puts it aside on his desk. Then he finds my rolls of film. He recognizes the universally known Kodak logo.

"What's this?" he demands.

Is he thinking of confiscating them?

I suddenly realize he would not know the difference between film and photographs. And photographs are innocent, because as everybody knows, all tourists take photographs.

"Some photos," I say innocently.

"Of what?"

"Myself, my camel, the desert."

"Of what in the desert?"

I answer him with the most innocent tourist photos I can think of. "Sand dunes, sunsets, sandstorms."

"What are you going to do with them now?"

I try name-dropping one last time.

"I'm going to give them to the consul to take to Canada ... " I instantly realize my mistake. Will he think I am using diplomatic immunity to get them out of the country because I am a spy? I cover my slip as best I can, by adding quickly, "... because they can't develop this type of film in Nouakchott."

He puts my rolls of film aside on his desk. Is he confiscating them now? I freeze like an animal who has to fight. There is no line that separates my life from my film ... from my book. Life's goal is death's death. Destroying my film means also destroying a part of me. Suddenly, with a cruel smile that reveals his real reason for stopping me, he gives me back the rolls of film.

"You can go."

December 16

I telephone my mother and father. I am relieved when I hear their voices. Nothing has happened to them. I hang up and think back to a conversation before leaving Canada, between my mother and I.

"Frank," she pleaded, "why do you have to go to the Sahara?"

What could I tell her so she would not suffer?

"Is it money, Frank? Do you have to go because you need money? If it's money you need, I'll give you mine," my mother pleads.

"Mom," I try to say kindly, "I'm a filmmaker. I'm going to the Sahara to make a film."

I lied. The truth had been a secret for four years. It had to remain a secret, especially from my mother and father. It would destroy them to know why I am here.

December 17

I have been depressed since I returned to Nouakchott. There is no line that separates my trip from my life. No progress means no trip, means no life. I have not felt alive.

December 18

There is no progress possible on buying the rest of my supplies so I can leave Nouakchott. I am too sick to do anything. Too nauseous and feverish from amoebiasis. Amoebiasis is caused by water or food that is contaminated with shit. I lie in a room at Tacha's, waiting uneasily for the deliriousness that will soon come. From past experience I know that when it comes, doubt will set in. To the core. Doubt so utter that I will doubt finishing this trip. Doubt finishing this book. Doubt that nothing is impossible. Doubt death's death. Doubt my life.

I lie here waiting for it to come. I will fight back, and tell myself over and over and over that the doubt is deliriousness, therefore it is not real. It will feel real, nevertheless. Devastating. Like dying must feel.

December 21

I arrive back at Magta Lahjar, near the end of the day. Only diarrhea lingers on from the amoebiasis. It is so good to know that tomorrow I will be able to start making progress! I go to see the young man I hired to take care of my camel while I was away. He tells me my camel's foot is injured and that I will not be able to leave tomorrow.

December 24

Three more days without any progress. My camel's foot has a long cut on the sole from riding him a lot over stones. I made this mistake because I did not realize stones hurt a camel. I have had his foot treated and was told not to ride him for a week. I will not wait this long. But I will not leave until the day after Christmas.

December 25

On Christmas day in 1983 I took my grandfather to my mother and father's like I did every year. It was a happy day, as always. Later that winter I was away on a two-month trip. When I returned home, my mother sat down with me and said very carefully, "Frank, I have bad news."

"What, Mom?"

"Gramps died."

My eyes shut and I could not control them. They were desperate to shut out and thereby prevent my grandfather's death. I knew I could not talk in sentences now, because they were too long to say without my voice shaking. If my voice shook, my mother would break down.

"When?" I breathed.

She hesitated. As if she was afraid her answer would break me down too. "On your birthday."

Yes, my mother knew my birthdays were always days that hurt me. She knew my birthdays would hurt me even more, from now on.

"From what?" I breathed again.

"Gramps died from pneumonia."

Pneumonia, I despaired, as I shook the sand off my sleeping bag. Pneumonia is not a fatal disease. My grandfather would not have died had I been a doctor. Had I not been a filmmaker, but a doctor. Had I been what I should be. Must be.

Life Without Death

A Sending Without Any Recipient

Yann Beauvais

Sometimes we wait a long time to discover a filmmaker's œuvre. This learning delay moves it into a different temporal sphere, removing it from the context in which it first appeared, and the work becomes autonomous. I discovered the films of Frank Cole as a result of a letter-writing exchange with Mike Hoolboom.

Mike sent me a DVD of Frank's two feature-length films, hoping to get my attention. The films intrigued, attracted or provoked me, and they always made me think. Their vision led me to look beyond autobiography and tourist films. Beyond the immediately intriguing interest of a first-person cinema that differentiates itself from models explored by the film diary in experimental cinema, the two films propose an investigation that starts from an obsession with death. Death as a life force, death past due.

A Life (1986) and *Life Without Death* (2000) create in the desert a mirage of death. The desert is a fascinating space (for believers, for example, is it not the place that, experiencing its essence, predisposes us to having our perception of the world transformed?) as well as a space that transforms our worldly existence. In the desert, living conditions, perilous at best, have often been, and continue to be, represented by westerners as a bottomless pit of tales that associate mystical experience and that of folly or loss of self, according to the stories and accounts that fluctuate between revelation and autobiography.

For the western man, the desert is a mirage that engulfs him in delectation. It is a pristine space to conquer, or to take complete control of. It is the ultimate frontier. It is the place where, faced with heterogeneity, an extreme otherness can prove to be an internal force, in which abandonment of all certainties can serve another truth, a transcendence... There, we find ourselves, reveal ourselves and lose ourselves.

Let us be frank... the two films are problematic on more than one account. And yet, the voice... There is a voice that makes itself heard through the entire film. It is a low voice that evokes so many others, from William Burroughs to David Wojnarowicz. The deepness of the voice greatly moves me and irritates me, too. It dramatizes images by moving them into the psychological realm, into a sphere that is too personal, that ends up sounding petty. In fact, it works against the image, it breaks the fascination that these landscapes have the potential to evoke. It serves to disrupt the beautiful desert images. The voice draws us back to the project. It signs and assigns images to a particular territory, that of a westerner who has undertaken a distant voyage in order to test himself. What is foretold is a voyage toward a death. We are far away from Werther's love pain; these sufferings belong to other inventories. How not to think of Fernando Vallejo and his brief returns to Medellín: the kingdom of death that is so well described in at least two of his novels.[1] The approach is daring, to the extent that the enthusiasm of the Colombian writer dialectically matches the asceticism, the gravity and the bombast of Frank Cole. All evidence suggests that we are not in the same realm; death is on the prowl, but are we really talking about the same thing?

The filmmaker gets lost in the desert. He is looking for the well shown on his map, but he doesn't find it. He passes dried-up wells, and a sense of unease sets in. The uneasiness increases; we are upset. In fact, we are as furious with ourselves as with the filmmaker who put us into this discomfort, because the sight of the diary film reflects the image of our meanness and pettiness back to us in whatever form they take. It is a painful experience, we would rather not have borne it, and yet...

The absence of these wells from the traveller's maps reminds me of the difficulty we have in accepting other ways of being in the world — this blindness to other ways of living, thinking and acting. Why should these wells be marked on his map? The demand is outrageous; it calls for the will of the white man to control and run the world — in other words, to dominate it, rather than to be in the world or of it. Such a demand cannot acknowledge the imponderable. Everything conforms to what is written.

But in this place change makes all the difference. It illustrates the wilful blindness that motivates this voyage. The desert is only a test. What is significant are the extreme survival conditions that it affords to a sick-at-heart westerner. We experience this irritation again when the filmmaker brings up the civil and tribal wars that took place in some of the lands that were crossed, to the borders of Chad and Darfur. For the filmmaker, these wars are an obstacle. The overbearing quest sees only what deflects it, whatever delays its plan to cross the entire length of the Sahara. The life and death of others (as long as it is not the grandfather) is only collateral damage. The perseverance of the project plunges us into a web of contradictory sentiments. It is fascinating, but it is also unacceptable. We are almost in a double bind. But this double bind shows how the contemporary forms of colonialism — or should we say neo-colonialism? — show themselves today. A reality is substituted onto the ones (not) encountered, masking one with a dominant one.

The project, the crossing, is stronger than everything. Anything that interferes with its completion, or even postpones it, is brushed aside, is evil. Everything has to make way for the project, even the filmmaker's body. Has he not spent months preparing so that he can endure this isolation? We are impressed by the irrepressible will that sets out to fulfill such an odyssey. We cannot help but admire the stubborn obstinacy of this blindness, while being unable to disregard its alienness.

This is not about filming the desert, let alone its inhabitants, whether they be villagers, nomads or other travellers. It is about relating an interior adventure. The guides are almost foils; they are uneasy, frightened. As usual, the Orientalist speaks for the Arabs, as Edward W. Said noticed: "Orientalist generalizations about the Arabs are very detailed when it comes to itemizing Arab characteristics critically, far less so when it comes to analyzing Arab strengths."[2]

What matters, and filming it bears witness to this, is the struggle of an individual facing extreme conditions. I cannot get it out of my head, however, that the experience had long ago been planned and decided. The film shows this in accordance with a production aesthetic and criteria that highlight its purpose — to know the solitude of a destiny. Therefore, the long away-shots along the sand-covered road when the adventure begins, or when he leaves one of these guides...

There is some complacency in how the trials are shown through the various sequences of body wounds. We are faced with an incredible exhibitionism that requires reactions that are contrasting, to say the least, and range from compassionate support to rejection.

We are within the effect. Distance no longer exists.

We have a complaint, a farewell song, that we need to belong. There is subtlety and outrage in the demand that makes me pass from irritation to rejection.

Although I am moved, I cannot bear to be used to this extent, as so many films do, each in their ways. In this regard, the music holds a special place. It conveys and recaptures the clichés of an exoticism shared by entertainment films that range from *Lawrence of Arabia* to *The Sheltering Sky*. We are in the kingdom of North African music stylings, revised and edited by Richard Horowitz. The music highlights the psychic state of the traveller and, finally, shows what separates us ...

No, I will not take this road. And yet, the film is questioning me.

Notes

1. *La virgen de los sicarios*, 1994, translated as *Our Lady of the Assassins*, Serpent's Tail, 2001, and *Mi Hermano el Alcade*, 2003.

2. Edward W. Said. *Orientalism*. Penguin Books, 2003.

Regarding Frank Cole
Ben Vandoorne

Our lives consist of encounters. They are the reason we exist, I firmly believe this now. Frank Cole, a name that no one around me is familiar with. Nevertheless, for me, someone who never knew or met him, he had, over the years, become close, a friend I talked to inwardly. May he rest in peace.

I lived in Egypt for seven years, sometimes coming back to spend a week or two in Belgium. Most of my time there I was bored. One stormy night I decided, oddly enough, to turn on the television. Just then, on a German network, a documentary was starting. *Life Without Death*. I remember it like it was yesterday. Beneath the nighttime lights and the repeatedly distorted images, I was absolutely hypnotized, as if someone or something were saying, "Look at me."

Several years passed, and then my destiny pushed me toward a certain path where Frank has come back to me even more forcefully than the first time. On a sudden impulse I decided to throw myself into an extreme adventure. An adventure that was to become a film I have called *Incha Allah* (87 minutes, 2007), a personal fiction in which I wanted to pursue a new confrontation with myself in the total isolation of the desert.

Thus, I organized and prepared over the course of a year. At first it was easy; between researching materials, applying for authorizations, and the physiological expenditure of my sports training, I was completely occupied. And then, abruptly, several weeks before the grand departure, what started as a mild doubt little by little became deep anguish. Sleep would not come and torpidity eroded me. This is when the sign occurred. Before writing this, I had never told this to anyone other than Claude Chamberlain, at our meeting in Montreal in 2007.

The sign came in a totally unexpected way. It took the form of a lost spam within my email. It is a spam that I have kept to this day, the sender of which was... Frank Cool. From that moment on, my doubts evaporated, and I understood that I would not be alone on my voyage.

My first confrontations, and my first nights alone in the desert, were at Wadirum in Jordan. Even today, my heart yearns for that particular desert. Those who know me will understand.

Sahara, in Arabic, means "desert." There are a number of ways we can exist in the desert. The first is physical, through the body and the senses. The emptiness and the immensity grabs attention; so does the light and harmony. The deep silence registers in the ears, and at the same time the slightest breath of wind moving the grains of sand makes one tremble. One can no longer tell whether the sound comes from several miles away or from just beside you. Then comes the cruelty of the desert: the heat, the long marches, the thirst, the wounds, the fatigue and dysentery. Lastly comes the internal confrontation. The contemplation that becomes a meditation on the self and on the world. Religiosity and mysticism.

There is a real fascination today for the desert. It arrives as a rejection of polluted, overpopulated cities, saturated with noise of every kind. The world needs to be freed from the pressures of our society, from the chokehold of everyday life. But the desert is also a hostile and dangerous universe that is not for everybody. It is not just beautiful sand dunes. In particular, it consists of rocks and rubble that you will end up cursing because of the way they twist your ankles. We take the desert as we take the sea, and with any departure, we have to cross the red line, the line we cannot step back from. From this point on, our only enemy is our own fear, and we have to overcome it. But let there be no mistake. There are, in fact, a number of deserts and the most dangerous is not always the one we think of first. There is also the desert of huge, overpopulated cities, the one we can erect between ourselves and other people. Behind everything, there is the most dangerous of them all, the one that has so often made me flirt with death, so as to better face life: the desert inside.

Crossing any of these deserts forces you to organize your possible risks, and to find the essential once more. Until a new way of looking at your life, and at life in general, and the beauty that surrounds it, emerges.

In the desert there are roads and paths. But the crossing does not truly begin until these roads and paths disappear. From then on, you are not crossing the desert, you are part of it. The desert is an ideal observation point for seeing ourselves more clearly. It is the heart of the world. You sense your entire being and the space surrounding you, and you wonder what brought you there.

You free yourself of extraneous things, and each of your actions becomes habitual, a kind of ritual to help you stay balanced. The kilometres pile up and you move according to the rhythm of the water holes shown on the map. During these efforts, you do not sweat; your body knows what it needs to do to retain water, that it must economize. But when the time comes to drink, after one sip you sweat profusely; you start to sniffle as if you were catching a cold. In seconds you are gorged, your head turns and your thoughts become clouded. Drunk on water…

I recall distant horizons. In the desert you have room. Tirelessly eating up the kilometres. Still advancing. Space in cities is not open.

When we film in the desert, we are always somewhat deceived. Because a screen is small. This is not what you really see. Sometimes I wished for someone beside me.

But in the desert, two is often too many. The desert is never silent. There is always something to listen to. The desert is hungry; it is eager to devour all traces of your steps in the sand. At this point problems occur. They may be more or less serious, and then you will feel the fear and anguish in your guts. There were difficult times when I howled my fear and distress, and moments of bliss when I sensed I was feeling the breath of God. As I write this, I have tears running down my face.

In the desert you can count only on yourself. And sometimes not even that. It is extreme situations that reveal us to ourselves. In these moments you have your modesty. In the desert, the greatest danger is not so much getting lost; rather, it is losing your head. Solitude can sometimes afflict like a sickness, like a cancer that takes over your entire being and devours you bit by bit. But this trial also causes you to discover who you were and catch a glimpse of who you could be. Crossing the desert is an intimate experience. An encounter with God, and with yourself. You think a lot in the desert. To yourself. There are also encounters. Encounters with faces branded by the sun, on which you can read the desert's soul. At last you reach the destination. My destination was not important. It was the undertaking that mattered.

But above all, beyond this story that I created from whole cloth, there was a presence. The presence of Frank, whom I sometimes asked: "Frank, what would you do in my place?" "Frank, did you feel that, too?"

Frank Cole's work has received far less distribution than it deserves. More than ever, the public has needed the example, the vision and the profound meaning that we give to our lives, which *Life Without Death* offers us and invites us to. May the media intelligentsia hear us.

When my film was at the Montreal festival, the founder, Claude Chamberlain, said to me, "Ben, you have helped me revive the memories of my meetings with Frank."

Yes, I will say it again: I sensed the presence, the soul of Frank Cole, around me. And as my Canadian colleague, Korbett Matthews, wrote to me so beautifully, "Yes, Frank is a phantom. He might even be a guardian angel."

Life Without Life (The Camels Are More Human)
Steve Reinke

A particular event in Cole's life serves as the impetus for both *A Life* and *Life Without Death*. This event, despite being repeatedly referred to, and depicted in both documentary and allegorical/symbolic fashion, remains sketchy, as sketchy as the biblical episode of Isaac and Abraham, which it inverts. At his beloved grandfather's deathbed, Cole briefly entertains the possibility that he would like to switch places, that he would sacrifice his life to save his grandfather's. This thought so unsettles Cole, he declares he must never die.

How unsettling this primal scene: the camera is already there, set up squarely at the foot of his grandfather's bed, pointing slightly upward so as to include the standing Cole, who splits his gaze between his grandfather and the camera. (But Cole's camera is always already there, anticipating every image, like Kubrick's camera. It isn't there to record, or to determine any kind of outcome or meaning, but to witness with an unflinching blankness the vaguely diabolical anticipation of an unconcerned participant.)

God called on Abraham to sacrifice Isaac, but it was only a test. Kierkegaard, in the "Exordium" to *Fear and Trembling*, retells the story in four versions: 1. Abraham turns wildly to Isaac and claims that it is his desire, and not God's, to kill him. Isaac pleads to God for mercy and is spared. Abraham claims: "It is better that he believe me a monster than he should lose faith in you [God]." 2. Abraham is about to sacrifice Isaac, but then sees the ram God has left as a substitute and slaughters that instead. "From that day henceforth, Abraham was old; he could not forget that God had ordered him to do this. Isaac flourished as before, but Abraham's eyes were darkened, and he saw joy no more." 3. Abraham begs God's forgiveness for the very fact that he had been willing to sacrifice his son. 4. Isaac sees Abraham draw the knife, and at that moment loses faith. "Not a word is ever said of this in the world, and Isaac never talked to anyone about what he had seen, and Abraham did not expect that anyone had seen it."

So, let's say Cole is Abraham and his grandfather is Isaac. (God is the camera.) *Pace* Kierkegaard, we could expand/interpret Cole's primal scene in various ways, but I find only one terribly convincing: A young man stands astride his beloved grandfather's deathbed. He imagines that if he could sacrifice himself and die in place of his grandfather, he would. He is immediately horrified by his willingness to sacrifice himself and vows to embrace life, a life without death. However, to embrace this life without death, he must first turn his back on his grandfather and disavow the (potentially sacrificial) love he had for his grandfather. At the risk of sounding trite: life without death is also life without life, though Cole remains oblivious to this fact, and is doomed to blankly, unknowingly diminish life.

Cole's films are shaped as quests for greater self-understanding, though it is clear that none is really sought. Even the slightest glimmer of self-knowledge will not break through Cole's determination to survive himself. How could it? A death drive as narcissistically driven as this doesn't leave room for hobbies. His is a quest away from subjectivity, life and love. Other possibilities: a spiritual quest, a geopolitical mapping, some kind of cross-cultural — or even cross-species — understanding. Well, it just doesn't happen. He goes through camels like tissues. (I'm exaggerating; actually, he goes through camels like handkerchiefs.)

There is a type of purity here, a cinematic purity beyond, say, Herzog. The purity comes from an almost complete abnegation. These films are blinkered to everything but Cole's radiantly mute and narcissistic death drive. The images are blanks, without any interiority or master narratives. The end of *Life Without Death*, when Cole has accomplished his quest and sits on the beach looking at the sea, would be even more hollowly anticlimactic were it not for our foreknowledge that his unacknowledged, but painfully obvious, quest for death succeeded in his subsequent Saharan holiday.

But how beautiful are his images. How beautiful are his images of desiccated corpses. They are the only thing he will vacate the shot for.

Film is for fetishism; video, narcissism. That's just the way it is, the way it used to be. Fetishism requires some kind of scene, room to move about, yearning over time, a shape to the ceremonies. Bodies, objects, transformation. There's just no room for any of that in video. In video, you can look at yourself, whisper to yourself, lulled in a steady-state feedback loop. Cole brings the narcissistic interiority of video to film as he demonstrates that narcissism survives (filmic) death, is stronger than death.

The dead animals are fetishes. They are film. Every image, roughly speaking, is either a Cole image or a corpse image, which is to say, all the images are of a piece.

But the audio, Cole's audio, is decidedly filmic: the sounds are so very far away from the images. I'm always disturbed by the use of foleyed audio in otherwise documentary film. I wish it were inverted; I wish we listened to the world and made up whatever images we wished. Foley: two guys stand in a little closet manipulating rattles and bits of metal. They look through the little window and crumple paper as — on the large, silent screen — villages burn.

Cole's sparse deployment of audio is as masterful, as formally tight, as his use of the film medium. He's really (I may have failed to mention) quite good. His use of foleyed sound is judicious, except for one sequence: the makeshift surgery in the Sudan. I take this sequence to be significant; certainly it is an anomaly in an otherwise tight film. It is the only sustained sequence that has neither Cole images nor corpse images. But it does have images of a Caesarean section (inverted corpse image) accompanied by ridiculously intrusive sounds of wet sucking and sloshing. The overly loud sounds break the documentary veracity of what otherwise would have been a viscerally intense scene. This grotesque foley betrays a comically sadistic view of reproduction.

And is it wrong of me to mention, after claiming the work is structured narcissistically, that Frank (may I call him Frank?) is beautiful? No, it must be mentioned, but mentioned and forgotten.

I Come Here for the Rites of Your Unworlding
Mike Cartmell

A man is crossing a desert. He is crossing the desert, and he is alone. He is riding a camel, alone, crossing the vastest desert in the world.

*

He is crossing the desert. His journey terminated by police in eastern Chad, due to the risk of fighting nearby, he finds himself drawn to the hospital. Drawn, he says, "to the struggle of life over death." Surgeons treat a person wounded in the conflict, and perform a rather perfunctory C-section, hauling an infant by the throat into the world. The child would be about eighteen now, if indeed it has survived the inexhaustible brutality of a world in which the category "children" intersects massively the category "victim."

And the category "killer."

This sequence occurs in a section of *Life Without Death*, the title of which powerfully resonates for a viewer in 2008: "El Fasher, Sudan" — the capital of North Darfur. No doubt children are being rudely born there too. Reaching El Fasher will for the first time lead him outside the Sahara, because taking the outside route will be more hazardous, and thus he "must take it, on principle." This is one of the marks of the resolve and determination that anger and frustrate local officials, and that he bears as a point of pride. Whatever waiver is necessary, he will gladly sign it. Danger will not cow him; it is precisely what he seeks, what the journey is about. Going outside the Sahara is beside the point because the Sahara is beside the point.

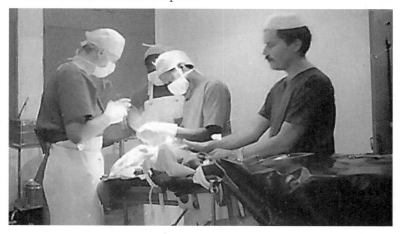

It has not been easy to write about the film of the man crossing the desert.

I see a word approach the desert.

It is not the word Sky or the word Earth. Neither the word Sand nor the word Seed, but the word Nothing, the word Void.

The desert confides only in the desert.

You realize and you do not realize you are disappearing.
(after Edmond Jabès)

A man is crossing the desert. I wish I could see him as a mythic creature, embodying the universal, containing multitudes.

I would hear him declaim:

> I am the colour of vastness.
> I am the burden of solitude.
> I am the tortured camelhoof.
> I am the milky wellwater.

I would separate him from his maker, about whom I know little, almost nothing, and about whom I presume to say nothing, or very little.
He would declaim:

> I am the throat in thirsting.
> I am the ruin and the shoring against ruin.
> I am the prisoner and the prisonguard.
> I am the boil in blister.

He fascinates, enthralls. Like a knight in some old-fashioned book. Not because he's undertaken the arduous, heroic journey, but because he's tilting at windmills. Well, not exactly: it's more complicated than that.
And he declaims:

I am a beetle for burrowing.
I am a seeker for hazard.
I am a bloated donkeycorpse.
I am a message that stuns me.
I am a torn trouserpocket.
I am a scorpion.

In Niger he receives an unexpected note from a French soldier (a Legionnaire?) stationed somewhere in the area. Its telling locution, improbable in address, impossible of response: "I hope you're alive." If only it were that simple.

I repeat the *beau geste* of its salutation, and call him "Franck."

And Franck declaims:

I disappear as a camelpath.
I flatten as a desiccated carcass.
I carry the ashes.
I am lost and guide the lost.
I am vacuous as the featureless landscape.
I go on ahead.
I sleep apart, alone.

*

Once another man, a younger man, a very young man barely become a man, was crossing a much smaller desert. He rode an old beat-up bus, not a camel. I was that man, and can recount my own paltry desert experience: somewhere between Lashkar Gah and Qandahar in Afghanistan, the bus had stopped at a watering hole, an oasis you might say, and everybody else had gotten off to relieve themselves, to get a drink or to stretch their legs. I don't know why but I stayed where I was, on a seat at the very back. It was ridiculously hot. A man appeared at the front of the bus and began to move slowly toward me.

Perhaps because of the heat, perhaps because it was Afghanistan, the rest of this, actions and thoughts, seemed to take place over a weirdly extended duration, as if in slow motion. I supposed that the man was a beggar. This was a rote response; beggars would get on the bus at every stop. But this man was different. He was dressed in blue, almost a sky blue (certainly not typical), his dhoti and turban were very clean (unusual for a beggar) and of fine fabric, silken, almost shimmering. He wore a blue silken cloth, a kind of veil, over the entirety of his face. The cloth was or seemed to be slightly moist. He came slowly down the aisle. There was a dawning double recognition that the man was about to show me what was under the cloth, and that I did not want to see it. My field of vision began to narrow and darken. I felt a swell of anxiety. I fished in my pocket for whatever change I had, and held it out at arm's length, saying something — pointless, pathetic — in hopes that he'd let me be. He came slowly forward. He took the money, made a wet throaty unintelligible sound that I for some reason interpreted as an expression of disgust, and turned to go; then he stopped, turned slowly back, and with a sort of flourish, removed his cloth. The movement of my scalp was palpable. I was barely nineteen at the time.

This is the only way I can put it: the man had no face.

*

"Distance is blue," said Tennessee Williams. I heard this from a colleague during a critique session at Ryerson many years ago when a student's photographs of a desert landscape were at issue. The line is from Williams' play *Camino Real*, occurring in the opening scene; the stage directions describe the first character who enters as being "dressed like an old 'desert rat.'"

Quixote [ranting above the wind in a voice that is nearly as old]: Blue is the colour
*   of distance!*
Sancho [wearily behind him]: Yes, distance is blue.

Blue is also the colour of nobility; Quixote goes on to assert that one should have a bit of blue ribbon about one's person, tucked in what remains of one's armour, or borne on the tip of one's lance. It would serve "to remind an old knight of distance he has gone and distance he has yet to go … "

At this point Sancho mutters "the Spanish word for excrement."

*

"I loved my grandfather. I'd have faced death for him if it meant he could live." Is this selflessness? Or the extremity of egoism? Or is it merely ordinary melancholia? On the border, as Freud says, of psychosis to be sure, but ordinary nevertheless, something most of us have experienced.

When a loved one dies, the loss is a hole that opens up in the Real. A flood of images rushes in, as if to fill the gap. Mourning would work to marshal those images, to subject them, without guarantee of success, to some form of symbolic constraint in a difficult, painful process of indefinite duration, not necessarily terminable since that hole, that absence, will persist. It is not uncommon to seek to short-circuit the process, and thereby circumvent the pain and difficulty, by

165

means of a fantasy of exchange: "Rather me than him." This fantasy also serves to assuage the guilt associated with loss: "Why him rather than me?"

In Franck's case, the profundity of the fantasy is writ large, since his offer of exchange is, on the face of it, so ludicrous. Why should a young man in his prime wish to die in the place of one so sick, frail and so very old? And, should the exchange be made, of what sort of life would Fred Howard be in possession? He would continue to be very old, frail and sick, still at death's door, soon to cross the threshold, and Franck would be dead. Unless Fred became Franck, assumed his life entire. But there's nothing rational about fantasy: it's unconscious and the unconscious doesn't obey the rules of rational thought, and so we're obliged to take Franck seriously. His ingenuousness in exposing his pathology is one of the reasons his film is so compelling, at least to me.

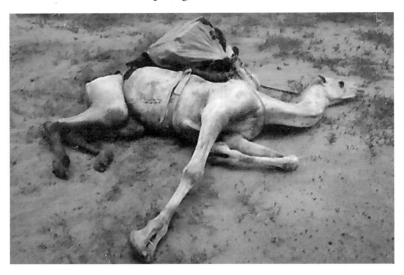

*

"It was my grandfather's death that made me decide to cross the Sahara desert by camel." This is given as the founding moment of the journey, and thereby of the film. No connection is established between grandfather and Sahara. Later we do see a photograph of a young boy, presumably Franck, mounted on a camel, but its provenance remains obscure. It eventually becomes clear that the Sahara is not the issue; it might as easily be the Arctic, some mountain, the bottom of the sea. What Franck wants is a trial, and his adversary will not be the landscape or environment, but death itself.

Franck is animated by, or perhaps at the mercy of, anxiety. I'll say this without presuming to know its specificity for him. He mentions particular moments of anxiety throughout the journey, but its most fundamental aspect is blocked, utterly occluded. We are twice given the images of the grandfather shaking in his hospital bed: frail, helpless, he is in the throes of death. The second, longer version has Franck walk from the bedside to the camera, apparently to turn it off.

Anxiety surges up in the presence of the dying person, in the presence of the cadaver. "I will be that" is its simplest formulation. We can parse it more subtly: the corpse establishes an uncanny relation between here and nowhere, between personhood and mere materiality; the other has been immobilized thus, and I know his demise in the silence I feel in my soul when I find myself continuing to address my private thoughts to him from whom my distress recognizes that

henceforth no response shall come; the cadaverous presence instills in me the foreboding of a death that shall not pass me by; I am mortified by the "unbearable image and figure of the unique becoming nothing in particular, no matter what." (Blanchot)

In Franck's world, we have instead the personification of death as a master against whom it is possible to struggle, against whom one can test oneself (if the test is sufficiently severe) and against whom one can, presumably, prevail. A master whom one can utterly vanquish if the trial is onerous enough. A master whose secret name is Fred and who lives in a little glass bottle with a cork on top.

Is it beside the point to mention that cinema in effect "cadaverizes" its human objects? To recall, after Bazin, Barthes and others, that its basis in photography entails a process of preservation, of embalming? Mummification: a desert technology. Part of what is so productive of anxiety, so remorselessly uncanny, in the images of Fred's death throes is that their persistence is guaranteed; we can always return to them, must always return to them, in the endless repetition without variation that is the cinematic form. The other part stems from Cocteau's slogan that the cinema "films death at work." In some sense we see this process literalized in Fred, who appears as an elderly but relatively healthy man, as a dying man seemingly moments away from the end, and as a box of cinders. But death works in cinema's essential temporality, in the mere succession of frames one after another; death comes creeping in the moment it takes Franck to say: "I loved my grandfather."

A man crosses a desert. He crosses a desert, then comes back and makes a film about a man crossing a desert. Then he crosses the desert again and he doesn't come back. We shall go to him, but he shall not return to us.

The obsessional neurotic's question, Franck's question, is (at the level of the *unconscious*: I am underlining that word) "Am I alive or am I dead?" Being dead means being utterly outside enjoyment; enjoyment that is concentrated in, embodied by, a monstrous other, a master. Being alive is the position of mastery; it is an excessive, all-too-enjoying, obscene aliveness, which overcomes the very register of lack, which is therefore the very lack of lack. A position of mastery that overcomes, or obviates, or erases, or annihilates death itself.

The paradox here is that, in Franck's fantasy, the position of the troubling, uncanny, obscene aliveness that annihilates death is occupied by Franck's only master, also death. Death is a master from Ottawa, in a corked bottle lying in its custom compartment in the camera case, and it is death that enjoys, death that exceeds, death that is truly alive.

"I forced myself to become a recluse, to become a person so alone that I could never be crushed by loneliness." Thus Franck's justification for the annihilation of the other, which is one of the defining traits of obsessional neurosis. But in the "Preparation" section, there is a drift into perversion, mostly in the form of fetishism, as well. The pervert is the one who works unceasingly for the enjoyment of the other, and the one whose outlook is unmitigated certitude. The "Preparation" section is fetishistic in style, with the high-con black and white, the heavily and obviously foleyed sound effects, the minimalist staging, and it contains multiple and thoroughly eroticized fetish items: the dagger, the belt and buckle, the naked chest. Finally, the bottle is filled with the grandfather's ashes.

Fetishistic belief is structured in the form of repudiation: *I know very well that* this is merely an ordinary bottle containing cinders, *but just the same*, it is for me the very substance of my lost loved one. And since it is the very one, the very other, my very master whose obscene living enjoyment compels my journey in the first spinning place, it must accompany me, guide me, protect me, preserve me as I seek to overcome my foe in holocaustic utter burn. Consumption, consummation. Devoutly to be wished.

At the same time, as it is the master it is my foe, it is what I needs must overcome, burn utterly. In being alive I am only dead; I am nothing, I am going nowhere, better I should be dead than him. In being dead he is unbearably alive, intolerably enjoying; he is everything, he will take me across millions of metres of desert, he overcomes and in overcoming must be overcome, I must become him. I must be the one who says, "I am become death, destroyer of worlds."

*

A couple of years ago, during one of innumerable car rides between Mobile and Buffalo, I told Jazzbo the story of the man in the sky-blue dhoti. This unleashed a ten-week barrage of questions (a barrage that has since dwindled to occasional sniper fire, but that, I fear, will never exhaust itself completely) because, as, to my chagrin, I eventually understood, the story has a structural and necessary lack in it, a fundamental incompleteness. The questions boiled down to one, really: what did his face look like? I can only say he had no face, even though I saw something; it seems beyond my capacity to describe what I saw except in terms of a nothingness. The story and its meaning had become, for me, a kind of metaphysical fable (lack of face = effacement = loss of self, of personality = loss generally = death), but try telling that to an eight-year-old.

*

When Franck initially mounts his camel and sets off down the road in Mauritania to begin his journey, waving back at a local man (and at the camera), he resembles Don Quixote in those famous illustrations (Matisse?). Shortly afterward, there's a shot of him crossing the frame left to right, in which he's the

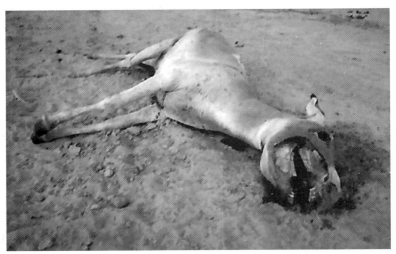

spitting image of a version of Sancho Panza that I think I saw as a doodle by Nabokov on one of the manuscript pages of his Cornell lectures on the novel.

*

Thinking is effacement, it attenuates the ego, edges toward the abstract and the general, which is to say, the human. Despite death's register outside experience, despite any locus of inquiry that might be canvassed for actual accounts, despite the resistance of death to symbolization as such, it is possible (if not necessary, if not absolutely [yes, pun intended] vital) to think it. Franck's thinking, however, amounts to little more than a vague articulation of his foundational fantasy (and it is worth bearing in mind here that whenever we enunciate the unconscious we inevitably render it vastly less complex and overdetermined than it actually is): I am haunted by death; my fear of death summoned me like a calling to the Sahara; I will confront death; I will fight back; I want life without death. Far from effacement, this approach places the self at the centre of the business, lets it loom large: we are repeatedly given Franck's face, or part of it, in close-up, to read the plainly written truths upon it.

The desert landscape, which he calls "featureless," is a garden of delights that quite properly ought to beckon to one, ought to compel an interested party to journey into, through and even across it. But from the moment he sets foot on the sandy Mauritanian beach, everywhere Franck (or his camera) looks the desert is covered with carcasses, flattened, desiccated, inert. Franck makes no grave metaphysical judgments. He simply makes a grave.

*

"Still haunted by death, nine years later he returned to the Sahara." It may be that I'm being too harsh in judging what may only be a tarnished and commonplace cliché. Perhaps we are merely witness to the harnessing of an inchoate but ineluctable response to an inevitable but occluded reality, like the awareness of equilibrium revealed at the moment we lose it.

But I don't think so.

In my view (contorted as it may be), this being "haunted by death" is either not as transparent and readily digestible as one might hope, or else it is far too transparent, and party to that species of "personification" or "anthropomorphization" that exists simply to render its object (death in this case) completely outside real intelligibility. It might be palatable, even comforting, to metaphorize death as an adversary against which we can struggle and even prevail, but we require (do we not?) art to give us something more. If this only is the result of the real enough encounters with death that the film depicts, if it is the limit of the insight to which those encounters give rise, then one would prefer it if *Life Without Death* was *actually* a film about a man crossing the Sahara desert alone by camel. It can only be imagined how a rigorous contemplation of (the full scope of) the desert landscape, its hideousness and its beauty, its proximity and its distance, its history and future, as well as a consideration of other obvious themes such as solitude, the journey, its risks and rewards, art, loss (there are no doubt numerous others) and even (dare I say?)

an actual engagement with the Saharan people, might have produced a film in which the journey, the desert, and Franck in it, could be seen directly and without let.

*

To philosophize is to learn how to die. (Montaigne, after Seneca)

*

Death eludes comprehension. It is what we cannot take hold of, what on the contrary comes to take us. That is, to take me.

If death is incomprehensible, it is not because it is invisible or intangible, unobservable, nothingness; it is because it is radically, irremediably singular. Ungeneralizable and therefore unconceptualizable, it is not unintelligible but rather the first intelligible, eminently understood in all understanding.

The understanding of the singular death makes understanding real, for all real beings are in the singular. What is intelligible is not first a singular being, the being that exists in the first-person singular, but the singularity of non-being, the incomparable and solitary absoluteness of nothingness unrelentingly closing in on me.

Nothingness cannot make sense, make itself sensed, except as a singular and unrepeatable catastrophe, in the specificity of my own destination for it.

*

Don Quixote's misfortune is not his imagination, but Sancho Panza. (Kafka)

*

The world is not a shelter from death; it is neither an arena within which we are to struggle against death. On the contrary, death is everywhere in the world; it is the world itself. The end, nothingness, is everywhere latent, and in opening the door upon the landscape of the world I open it upon the abyss.

In advancing down the pathways of the world, I very certainly go to my death. With one and the same movement existence projects itself, fascinated, into the world and projects itself, anxiously, unto its death.

The movement of existence is not the stalwart advance of some shining knight upon his steed, armed with a lance tipped with a ribbon of blue, shielded by a perverse certitude; it is, as Heidegger puts it, a groping.

*

Kafka's fragment "The Truth About Sancho Panza" deserves quotation in full, as it is so delightfully brief:

> Without making any boast of it Sancho Panza succeeded in the course
> of years, by feeding him a great number of romances of chivalry and
> adventure in the evening and night hours, in so diverting from himself
> his demon, whom he later called Don Quixote, that this demon there-
> upon set out, uninhibited, on the maddest exploits, which, however, for
> the lack of a preordained object, which should have been Sancho Panza
> himself, harmed nobody. A free man, Sancho Panza philosophically
> followed Don Quixote on his crusades, perhaps out of a sense of respon-
> sibility, and had of them a great and edifying entertainment to the end
> of his days.

Here Don Quixote, lost though he may be, is only a puppet. It wasn't he who spent a lifetime reading tales of knight-errancy and losing himself in febrile daydreams. Rather it was Sancho, who quickly grasped that those tales, with all the demons they aroused, would kill him in short order. And since Don Quixote didn't exist, Sancho had to invent him. Don Quixote was the name Sancho gave to the demon that dwelt within him, and whose destructive rage he required to "divert from himself."

Once the demon had found a name and become a character, its excesses no longer had to be suffered. Instead, Sancho could observe it from a certain distance.

Distance is blue.

*

The impotence of my death discloses to me my impotence with regard to my birth. Destined to death, delivered over to being: such is the specific nature of my passivity, the passivity of existence, affected by things and afflicted with itself.

To be delivered over to being is to be delivered over to death. It is to be subject to things, not only as a subject in which their refracted attributes can inhere, but subject to them, exposed to their forms and their qualities but also to their force and their aggression, mortified by them. It is an essential mortal structure that is expressed in our taste for the colours, our ear for what is intoned across the fields of being, our appetite for the honey and the lees of the day.

*

So Don Quixote, personified raging demon, undertook "the craziest exploits." Sancho was free to resume a contemplative life of modest interests (is this what we call philosophy?), while following, out of responsibility, his creature.

This fable suggests to me a sort of "royal road" to sublimation, whereby the invention, creature, puppet (artwork?) is invested with the destructive, enjoying, all-too-alive impulses within the subject, so that they may play out, harming nobody; so that they may be observed from a distance; so that their vicissitudes may be subject to contemplation.

As if the alternative would be fatal.

*

I like to encounter what I call "moments of unwatchability" in films. There's one in Phil Hoffman's film *passing through/torn formations*, with the video image of Phil's mum translating the voices of the Polish relatives as they tell the story of Uncle Janek's murder by his son. An example from the (relatively) dominant cinema would be the highway rest-stop encounter between Vincent Gallo and Cheryl Tiegs in Gallo's *The Brown Bunny* (not to mention the infamous blowjob

sequence from the same film). Myriad others could be adduced. These are moments that arouse acute discomfort in the viewer (or maybe it's just me), decentering, mortifying him, overwhelming in some sense his capacity to grasp them aesthetically (or any other way).

I find these moments compelling, can't turn away. They're like men without faces.

Here it's the sobbing scene. Right at the beginning of the film, shot from a weirdly high angle (who is there? who is shooting? how could anybody shoot this?), the sobbing Franck is clearly not the bedside Franck we've just seen; he's much older, and in retrospect it would seem that this scene was made after his return from the desert. Is this a performance, or a genuine moment? If the latter, why is the grief so persistent? Is it the same grief? Did Franck set up the shot, or is there in fact somebody else present? Why show this? Does it, or is it meant to, underwrite the loss that Franck articulates in various ways throughout the film? And so on.

The answers to these questions are unknown, and for me irrelevant. The violence of the grief, the heaving naked belly and chest, the erotic volume: I am pierced by the sobbing scene, tasked and heaped by it, find it repulsive and over-the-top, precisely unwatchable.

And thus utterly fascinating.

*

A man crosses a desert. He crosses a desert and then returns, and makes a film about a man crossing a desert. And then he returns to the desert, and then he doesn't return.

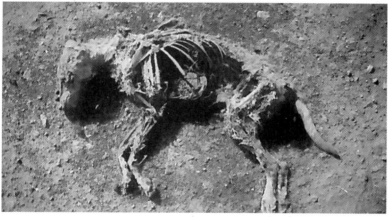

Hors texte: I've tried to be scrupulous in taking the film on its own terms, but I'm not immune to what's available to be gleaned from the internet. So I beg this one indulgence: it seems that after being found murdered in Mali, the film-maker's remains were not returned home to Ottawa, but instead were "cryogenically preserved at the Michigan Cryonics Institute in suburban Detroit's Clinton Township."

I don't know if this is true. But it is the stain on the garment, the remnant, the irreducible remainder that exceeds any possible closure of account.

And then he returns to the desert, and then he doesn't return.
And then he returns.

*

With Melville, Franck seems to be saying: "I've made up my mind to be annihilated."

*

If a mortal force of life can still assemble and steer itself, it is because it makes contact with a ground, a density of being closed in itself, the supporting element of the terrestrial. Precarious, fortuitous, the grain of substances takes form under the hand, the opaque still sustains the palpitation of the gaze.

Beneath the general and abstract outlines of the recurrent things, a mortal clairvoyance discerns the unrecurrent, the ephemeral, the fleeting; it discerns a field of chances, understands real beings, which are in the singular. The singular death imminent about me takes form in the singular constellation of possibilities, instrumentalities, chances and snares which form the singular landscape of the sensible world arrayed for me.

*

So, are you saying that art has to be philosophical?

No, I'm saying it should strive to protect us from, or at least alert us to, (our own) aggression and affliction, bear itself responsibly in the world, maintain a certain distance and provide instances of great and edifying entertainment, in the full sense of that word.

If we learn from it how to die, so much the better.

*

There came a day when the old knight Don Quixote, while reminding himself of the distance he had gone, no longer needed reminding of the distance he had yet to go; he succumbed to a fever which had kept him in bed for six days, during which time Sancho Panza, his good squire, never left his side.

Life Without: On the Film *Life Without Death*

Julie Murray

In his 1960 novel, *The Woman in the Dunes*, Kobo Abé describes sand thus:

> ...sand is sand wherever it is, whether from a beach or desert... (T)he size of the grain... shows very little variation and follows a Gaussian distribution curve with a true mean of one-eighth millimeter. Air or water currents set up a turbulence. The smallest wavelength of this turbulent flow is about equal to the diameter of the desert sand. Owing to this peculiarity, only the sand is extracted from the soil, being drawn out at right angles to the flow. If the cohesion of the soil is weak the sand is sucked up into the air by light winds, which of course do not disturb the stones or clay — and falls to the ground again, being deposited to the leeward.

Abé then goes on to describe the particulars of sand's behaviour in the aggregate, that it is the antithesis of all form, a shape-shifting menace that devours everything, the only certain factor its movement. "(It) didn't even have a form of its own... yet not a single thing could stand against this shapeless destructive power."

As the captive Niki fails again and again to escape the pit he has been lured into, the sand becomes ever more monstrous and invasive to the point where it seems to have entered his body and courses where his very blood does. It encrusts his eyes and the corners of his mouth, and abrades his skin, which breaks and bleeds. He vacillates between rage at its persistent incursion and slack acceptance of it as a new and inexorable condition of his life. This complex picture of sand deepens throughout the novel to become a living metaphor for the unfamiliar anxiety and fear Niki experiences as his firm ideas about liberation and stasis are all but inverted. His confusion is exacerbated since it never becomes clear to him which incidents or perspectives in the evolving events are suitable for hope and which for despair. Agonized by his captivity, he imagines the crumbling, rotting house as a ship, floating on the sand. In it one is always mobile, going somewhere.

Niki dreams about a pair of barrels as his vessel, one inside the other and hinged like a gyroscope, but this vessel includes neither a means of propulsion nor any kind of rudder. He spends the entire novel down in the sand hollow with an unnamed woman in a collapsing house battling the great quantities of sand that fall daily into the pit.

Frank Cole's encounter with the forces of this same substance involved circumstances that were in most ways the diametric opposite of those in Abé's story. Unlike Niki, Cole's survival depended on his constant mobility. His year-long push across the great sands of the Sahara is a practical manifestion of Niki's structure that can float on sand, ride its waves and currents and always manage an even keel, though Cole's means were a lot more traditional and dependable. He started out on the west coast, in Nema, Mauritania, and made his way through Mali, Niger, Chad and the Sudan, until he reached the Red Sea on his eighth camel.

His film about this extraordinary endeavour, *Life Without Death* (2000), begins with a spare synopsis of the four-year period of preparation preceding the journey, during which he disciplined his mind and his body, a period when, he informs us in uninflected voice-over, he deliberately sought isolation so that loneliness in the desert would not be the thing that killed him.

In the film, his apartment and his circumstances assume the emptiness of a desert long before he ever climbs a camel, something he does with the strength and evident physical discipline of an athlete. Interested in how one gets by in these parts of the world, I hitch a ride on his caravan of blind faith — which I gather wobbles nearly as often as the fiercely heated air he moves through — and live vicariously the fear he experiences directly. I never meet him, although he tells much about himself and is in the frame as often as not, on or off his mount.

In squarely composed shots, the viewer is presented with the preparation's itemized accounting: Cole in an otherwise empty room hoisting weights, pacing around his Steenbeck while teaching himself Arabic from a book, sleeping in an empty room, interviewing himself. From the beginning we understand that each shot and its set-up, while documentary, is at the same time a dramatic construct. One example of this deliberation is the lighting arrangement and noirish angular framing he employs as he films himself sharpening his knife, a long, anciently tapered dagger that, in a pool of furtive light, he drives against the sharpening stone again and again. Each movement is rigidly choreographed and measured, its meaning a succinct encapsulation of the information he wishes us to know. Nothing in these scenes is extraneous or left to chance. Except, of course, for the year spent crossing the desert.

The next time we see this kind of chiaroscuro is during an operation filmed at a hospital in Chad, closer to the end of his journey. A German doctor working at the hospital permitted him to film while helping him procure visas to continue travel in the area. The change of scene is shocking. The viewer is pulled from the broad and blistering light of the desert and thrust deep into darkness, into the interior of the body itself, as scalpel cleaves belly and gloved hands dig among livid tissue, extracting the baby during a C-section. This is a rare and visceral encounter with a fundamental force of life wildly outside his control.

At the film's beginning there is a shot of Cole's empty apartment, but it's not clear whether he has recently packed up or it has always been like this. Nobody comes to visit. There are no goodbye scenes, or scenes of waiting in line at busy offices for visas and vaccines. In dry, unadorned statements, he informs his invisible audience about the nature of his quest, but even that is not entirely clear. He seems bent on cheating death, but is attracted to it at the same time. He shuffles a ream of formal-looking papers and stands up from the table. The camera approaches the top sheet. Such is the established mood of the film that it could as easily be a last will and testament as what it is: The Retardation of Aging and Disease by Dietary Restrictions. Only in the west.

While his grandfather trembles uncontrollably in the end stages of life, Cole states flatly that he would willingly give up his own life if only it meant his grandfather could live. This, and the final shot of the film (not of the wide expanse of the newly encountered Red Sea, as one might expect, but of Cole's face looking upon the scene, uttering, "Alive!") offers a clue as to the trajectory Cole has set himself up for. One might think that such an undertaking would, by its extreme nature, cleanse the body and soul of grief, but it seems in that moment, instead of euphoria, Cole is experiencing something else. Maybe baffled disappointment. It is poignant, extreme and absurd all at the same time.

His second guide, employed to take him through Niger, is an Arab in a region where there is factional fighting between Arabs and the nomadic Tuaregs. This man endures sleepless nights of unrelenting fear before he finally turns back. Cole describes how, as they rode together, the guide became sick and was forced to walk. He expresses his admiration for this sixty-five-year-old man who made the 300-kilometre "physical feat" while in pain and urinating blood. Cole sees it as "defying old age, defying death." He assumes the guide is in pursuit of the same objectives as Cole himself, and is not simply a man trying to save himself, obligated to what Werner Herzog once referred to as "the monumental indifference of nature." Cole may be remembering his own grandfather, and his heroic take on this event might be the expression of his anguish at being unable to forestall the inevitable, a sorrow it appears he can never escape. This is not the first, nor the only time in the film when there seems to be something oddly unrealistic in his perception of the world. Odd, because, while he is expressing these thoughts, he is obligated himself to that very nature and witness at all times to its blind and brutal reality.

In spite of his admitted anxiety within this place, the desert is irresistible in its beauty and challenge, so clearly evidenced by his cinematography. Cole manages to pause regularly in order to construct with his camera some symbolic realities-within-realities. He stages numerous walk-ons with his camels. He frames apparent departures through the arched branches of dead trees. In a curiously premeditated shot, he has set up his camera to film himself off in the distance tugging at his clothing, while in voice-over he describes losing control of his body as a result of abject fear. He dreads not being able to find the wells marked on his ordinance survey map and discovering roads obliterated by the desert sands.

To see the kindness of reality requires an awful lot of beauty. The way Cole frames the landscape and attends so closely to that which composes and inhabits it — rock and sand, beetle and scorpion, and occasional dried salt beds — makes it clear he has been ladled plenty of this unquantifiable stuff to fortify him along the way. He films under a full moon. The dark powdered blue is like no other and the landscape is a curved penumbra holding the night like a bowl of milk. It is dark and it is light. Occasionally, he comes upon and films dunes of sand that have blown themselves into supine forms, one merging into the next, all the way to the edge of an imaginary bed. Just as a body would turn in its sleep, so do these hills swap themselves for something else in the dark, so that whatever peak a traveller might have pegged his survival on before the sun went down is guaranteed to have shifted during the night. Cole uses compass and map, and his camel follows dutifully along.

Perhaps time, the only thing he has plenty of, is the least formidable element he is facing, in spite of the urgency of his situation. It is an element whose abundance allows him periodic respite in such austerity. The length of any day, whether it brings unendurable boredom or unrelenting threat, is necessarily abbreviated in the film form, so that, for the viewer at least, his encounters with the circumstances of the Sahara seem to shift abruptly.

Flat horizons, rare cloud cover, grass scrub and any number of animal skeletons come under the gaze of the camera, a gaze not so much contemplative as calculating. At other times the subject and its arrangement are startling in their composure, so carefully and precisely framed, and serving nothing but the subject's beauty. It is during these moments that the viewer is permitted unmediated access to something of the awe of the Sahara, its structure and inhabitants.

Sound is captured along with image, and the wind, in its infinite, harmonious variety, often becomes the substance of the scene before us. It whistles under

pressure or groans deeply, raising sudden spinning cones of sand whipped into entities that seem alive for short, sudden moments. Otherwise, sounds in this flat open space are heard in isolation and without echo. The soft thumps and quiet crunch of sand that accompanies the walking camel contrasts with the lighter version attending the man. It is so quiet one would think the man would be tempted to talk to his camel. We hear the hissing of a snake suddenly happened upon, and occasionally the high-pitched scree of birds tearing the sky along its edges, but nothing else. No airplanes, small or large, ever pass overhead.

The music in the film, composed by Richard Horowitz, contributes to the gravity and momentum of the camels, in a deeply resonant score that fills the landscape and measures the great arc of the sky as it throbs in the depths of our bodies. These interludes of great relief describe something of the interior rhythm that our traveller must have experienced with a similar sense of unnamed optimism. More than occasionally, one hopes. The body singing to itself could never die of loneliness.

Meanwhile, the camels bear the aloof expression of the perennially unperturbed and exhibit no haste unless forced. These bad-tempered beasts are magnificent in their obdurate resistance and, moments later, impassive compliance, as they heave to their knees and then onto their platter-like feet. Their long limbs terminate in great, doughy pancakes. They bellow loudly, mouths agape. Somewhere I learned that camels can aim and spit a date stone as accurately as an archer launches an arrow, and can close their nostrils at will in a sandstorm.

They rest with their legs neatly tucked beneath them, compact as a log. Periodically, Cole films while riding. The camel's head bobs at the bottom of the frame, floating as if swimming and swaying from side to side, absorbing its surroundings. Its stride is so long, the ground moves beneath it in slow motion. We get a sense of the relative size of things when Cole, camera at shoulder level, films in close-up the thin white legs of the camels as they pass through the frame one by one. The large, woody knots at their joints give them the appearance of trees.

This creature seems instinctively inured to its place in the desert, regardless of the outcome, whereas Cole seems earnestly alien to it, and one can't help but feel that is not a good thing. It is impossible to turn one's eyes away, however, because in spite of this, Cole really does overcome adverse conditions and manages to cross the Sahara by camel alone. He was the first western person ever to accomplish this. He may get to keep the title for the foreseeable future since the world's deserts are expanding apparently without pause and becoming ever more inhospitable in the process, even to those people ancestrally acclimated to the extremes of temperature and lack of shade. Sand is quickly becoming the dominant feature threatening to swallow everything. What I imagine to be the old-fashioned desert — with which inhabitants of hundreds of years have long since developed a nuanced and fertile relationship, one not so bleached and featureless and one that supports life — is itself being swallowed. The hottest place on earth is getting hotter. Today's archaeological digs in the Middle East can only occur in the first few months of the year, as the temperatures in that region routinely reach life-threatening levels. The crowded streets of the city of Beijing are subject every year to a particularly pernicious yellow smog as airborne sands of the advancing Gobi invade and the fingers of the desert dunes move slowly nearer, like a larcenous hand across a table. These events last longer each year and are lately accorded the expectancy of seasons, they are so punctual.

October 9, 1990
I switch from following the vehicle path to following the railroad. It's straighter and shorter. It reminds me exactly of the railroad in the film *Lawrence of Arabia*. In fact, I've been reminded of *Lawrence of Arabia* all across the Sahara, because of the countless times while riding that I've recited the dedication poem that begins his book *Seven Pillars of Wisdom*, which the film is based on. Though the dedication poem's tragedy has brought tears to my eyes while riding, it has also brought tears of hope. After all, our desert campaigns arose out of the same reasons. Lawrence explains his purpose in the first four words of his book: "I loved you, so ... " Each day I recite this dedication, adding, "Dear Gramps." The death instinct causes man to want to die. In my war with death, the greatest loss was the day I realized that it is an almost solitary war. Lawrence's poem fills me with hope.

October 10
I have never told your only child, my mother, that I didn't bury all of your ashes. I secretly kept a vial and buried the rest. I couldn't let you go. This is why I've carried your vial all across the Sahara. Gramps, now you live with me.

October 11
I run into a small eating place beside the vehicle path. A pot of millet is cooking on a fire outside. There aren't any customers right now. As I ride by I peer into the hut and see there are no adults there. Two little boys, about eleven and six, are running it. The boy of eleven comes out and calls after me to come back for a tea. I ride back. The stimulant will help me with the morning's ride until I can make a few coffees at lunch.

He receives me like a man. We shake hands. He takes me inside the hut to sit down to rest on a cot in the shade. He makes me a tea. He asks me if I'd like some millet but I tell him all I need is the tea. I drink it gratefully, feeling better with every sip. I know he's not going to let me pay. He doesn't ask me a lot of questions because that's not what he's asked me here to do. What he's doing is his duty as a Saharan to treat me like family. But what has struck me the most about him is that he's not afraid of me. Most children are. A white man on a camel is an intimidating sight because they've never seen one before and because I'm filthy, and wearing torn clothes, and I carry a knife. I admire this little boy. There is nothing I admire more in people than courage. I shake his hand goodbye. Though I do not plan to have children, if I ever did, I'd love a little boy like him. I'd call him "Sahara."

October 12

Courage is something I have tried to teach myself for many years. This began in 1978 with my film teacher Peter Evanchuck, who tried to tell me that it was a person's most important quality. For two years he constantly called me a coward. I'll always be grateful to him. This made him the only person in my life who had a big influence on me.

I just keep pushing myself as hard as I can. Following the railroad from station to station, I don't have the two main dangers of getting lost or running out of water. Fatigue is what I have. I always have. For the first time on this trip I'm counting the days. I'm not able to count forwards because I don't know exactly when the end will be, so I count backwards from Khartoum. At least it allows me to count.

The new camel is also tiring. He's only walked 475 kilometres. Two days ago, when we ran into a big rain puddle, he drank for fifteen minutes straight! Much longer than I've ever seen any camel drink. I'm worried about him. This is why I dreamt last night that I was forced to slaughter him personally. I slit his throat with my knife, as is the Saharan method. I felt terrible about having to do it. Nightmare.

I drink three coffees with lunch. I could keep drinking coffee on and on and on, but now I force myself to start loading the camels again.

October 13

I wake up having slept poorly overnight because of another nightmare. Today I'll have to force myself a little harder through the fatigue. I can't remember what it was about. I don't have to. The only kind of nightmares I have are ones about death.

October 15

It doesn't matter that, without nightmares or mosquitos, I got my best sleep in a week last night. By 10:40 a.m. I have to stop for lunch to rest. I feed the camels one of the two big bundles of grass from beside the Nile that I bought to give them more strength. They devour it. I devour lunch. I've devoured every single meal I've had since I started my trip. It helps me start to recuperate. It makes me realize again, for the hundredth time, how hugely food has contributed to my success. Except for death, nothing has motivated me more to keep going than food. The pleasure of food is that great. I have lived for food. Lived for it. All across the Sahara I've helped myself through every morning's ride by telling myself, just a few hours to lunch. Now I reload the camels. Just a few hours more to dinner, Frank.

October 16

I'm relieved I'm able to get all the food I need, except sardines, in a town called Ed Damer. Noodles, dates, onions, peanuts and powdered milk. In the afternoon in a town called Atbara, I find sardines. Sudan is the only country where I haven't been able to get the food I need. There is a food shortage because of an economic crisis. People would expect me to lose weight from the exertion of this trip. I have actually gained a couple of pounds, due to the huge amounts of food I eat. I almost always eat 2,000 calories every day in dates alone, not including everything else.

October 17

The new camel is too exhausted to go further. By mid-morning he started to drag a little. I didn't pay much attention to it. My past camels walked a long distance after starting to drag. But by mid-afternoon he suddenly starts dragging hard. It's a strain on my own camel to drag him. First I try slowing down, but it makes no difference. Then I try riding him, thinking he'll walk faster with me kicking him. But he walks slower than a child. I have to kick him constantly to keep him going at all. I realize that the moment I stop kicking him, he's going to stop. A few minutes later I do stop kicking him. Like a car that's just run out of gas, he slowly comes to a stop. He just stands there exhausted. We just stand there.

October 18

As we stood there yesterday the first reaction I had was to look at my watch. Still an hour to go before dark and there's nothing I can do about it but camp. I realize this first reaction says everything about me. My mother and father once told me that when I was a little boy, I often told them that I didn't have enough time. Now I had a camel that was too exhausted to go on, but what was harder for me was losing one hour.

I didn't double-hobble him, so he could eat all night, and hopefully get a little strength back. I wasn't afraid of him running away; he was too exhausted for that.

This morning I switch his load for my camel's lighter one. Turning back to Atbara is out of the question because it's turning back. I'll try to get him another

160 kilometres to Musmar, the closest village, because it will be easier than trying to sell him at one of the railway stations along the way that usually have only a few people living around them.

Seven kilometres later he suddenly starts dragging hard. Three and half kilometres later he's dragging so hard I stop early for lunch, afraid he'll collapse if I don't. I sit him down and unload him so he can rest easier while grazing. But he doesn't stand up with the other camel to graze from the tree we're camped under. He sits for the next two hours in a stupor. Afterwards, as I film myself leaving in a mirage, I don't sit him down to rest as I'm setting up the camera, in case he can't stand up again. Getting him to walk the remaining 150 kilometres is impossible. He'd die.

October 19

I'm at a station called Dogwaya, which I arrived at yesterday afternoon. I'm waiting for an empty truck to come along to take my camel and travel ahead to Musmar or back to Atbara, to sell. The couple of trucks that have passed have all been full. The stationmaster says it's not allowed to put him on a train. There are so few people living here I couldn't find a buyer. A guy of about twenty offered to take my camel to Atbara on foot, 55 kilometres back. I told him no, that the camel could die before getting there.

He's emaciated. I've bought him a big bundle of millet stalks but it will take a month of doing nothing except eating for him to recuperate. Yesterday morning, to give him a little more time to eat, I decided to get caught up on filming. As I was starting, a short distance away from my camp, I heard pecking. I left my camera equipment and walked back to my camp. There was a hole pecked right through the plastic jerry can holding my stove naptha. The bird must have been very thirsty and thought it was water. Luckily I stopped the bird before all the naptha leaked away. I wouldn't have a stove for the rest of the trip. Then I covered up all my baggage with groundsheets, to be safe in case birds came back. I went back to continue filming. I find that my small pouch of camera accessories has been dropped a few metres away. Another bird must have been very hungry and tried to fly away with it. Luckily the bird wasn't big enough to lift it, otherwise I'd have only one of my three lenses to finish the rest of the trip with.

I remember the day, July 26, that I arrived in Sudan. From my saddle I looked east toward the Red Sea and tears came to my yes as I said out loud, "I'm coming home." I thought by now I'd faced everything the Sahara had, and Sudan would be easy. I was wrong. Of all the five countries, Sudan has been the hardest. Almost eleven months and 7,000 kilometres across the Sahara, I still have new problems. Yesterday's incident was so typical. The last thing in the world I expected to jeopardize my film was birds. The problems of crossing the Sahara are endless. What's next?

October 20

I more or less give my camel away, so I can keep riding. He's worth $700 healthy but I sell him for $50. I realized it didn't merit the time to take him to Musmar or Atbara since he's worth so little in his condition.

It also isn't worth buying another camel so close to the end. I'll try to get my other camel the last 350 kilometres. He's tired. He's already walked 1,800 kilometres, farther than any other of my camels, except the Malian. It'll be even harder for him now, because he has to carry most of the second camel's baggage. All I can leave behind is a saddle and a jerry can.

I leave. Though from time to time on the horizons I can see bushes, I actually pass only one group of bushes in 20 kilometres until I finally have to give up finding grazing to stop for lunch to rest. I've never seen so little grazing before. The only priority ahead of grazing is shade for rest and I've stopped in the excellent shade of a railroad car, at a station I've come to. My camel has nothing to eat, so he can recuperate.

He's had a big abscess on his side for a long time, which is bleeding a little now. I unload him completely, except for his saddle. He sits down and starts to regurgitate.

It turns out to be a longer day for him than it should. At sunset, as I'm starting to camp, a heavy rainstorm suddenly begins north of me. Then a couple of twisters emerge out of it, moving toward me in a line. I get back on my camel. I can't get a good enough sleep in my tent because I have to lie on my baggage to get off the flooding ground. Were it not for the unmistakable railroad track, I wouldn't be able to see to ride after dark. It rains a few drops, but I avoid the storm and the twisters. But I keep going because I don't trust that there won't be another storm overnight. After three and a half hours I arrive at a station called Ogein. I camp outside a building for shelter if necessary. My camel is tired. But I can't let him graze because I'm too tired to stay up any longer. In the dark I don't even know if there is any grazing. I give him a little seed that a kind man at the station gave me for him. My camel devours it in ten minutes. It's not nearly enough.

October 29

Pulling him isn't easier today. He's more exhausted than yesterday. My knee is still slightly sore. My feet are a little sore too. Though I put pads inside my shoes, my feet are sore enough that I still have to walk gently whenever there are stones. I'm tired by lunch, though I've pulled him only nine kilometres. I was a little tired before I'd even started from filming for two and a half hours. In the afternoon, I pull him 11 1/2 kilometres. Slow progress today. Sunset is at 5:30 p.m. now. I always need to go to sleep as fast as possible. I eat, tie up my camel six metres away in case of thieves and get into my sleeping bag by 7. I'm so tired I fall asleep in a couple of minutes.

Forty minutes later I wake up, and automatically look to check my camel is there. He's gone. Though a tied-up camel can still hop away slowly, he's too exhausted. I realize instantly he's been stolen. I realize I was right to take the recent warnings about thieves seriously. I look at his footprints with my flashlight. There are a man's footprints beside them. They are heading where I knew they would: away from the sand toward the stony ground. As soon as they get to it, there are no more footprints to follow. I come back. I follow his footprints the other way, and see he spied on me from behind a bush first. I realize how he was able to steal him without my waking up. By waiting for a truck to go by on the road, which has been running beside the railroad for the past three days, he covered up the sound of my camel moving.

I'm still a little scared that he could come back and kill me in my sleep, because he may be mentally ill. This is a small possibility because a thief who steals an animal in the Sahara is risking his life. He may be shot and killed if pursued. I pack my film and diary into a handbag, and head with my sleeping bag toward a hut I had made a mental note of before night fell. I find it abandoned. I realize the campfire I spotted here before must have been the thief stopped for dinner. I walk back to my camp and lie down again. Ten minutes later I get up, take my film, diary and sleeping bag, and hide myself up a nearby cliff.

October 30
A little before dawn, I go back to my camp. The thief didn't come back. My baggage is all there. I fill a pack with the minimum I'll need in food, clothing and film equipment to finish the last 75 kilometres on foot. Then I stop a truck and he drives me and all my baggage to the next village called Sinkat, four kilometres away, where I realize there'll be police to leave my baggage with while I'm gone. I explain to them what happened. They tell me to wait until they can go see where the camel was stolen.

It's 11:30 a.m. when the police and the tracker and I leave. I show them the footprints. The tracker, a civilian about 25 years old, starts following them on foot with two of the police. The other policeman and I wait 45 minutes, then follow. We find them waiting for us at the next small village, Summit, eight kilometres from where he was stolen. The tracker has lost the tracks here.

We drive back to Sinkat. They take me to a Scandinavian aid organization in the village, explain what has happened to me and ask to borrow a good jeep to track the thief. They kindly lend it to us.

At 2:30 p.m. we drive back to where the tracker lost the tracks at Summit. He's already asked around if anybody saw a man on a camel go by last night. There is a paved road here, which the tracker tells the driver to change directions and take. I realize he's thinking the thief may have turned onto the paved road, so he'd leave no footprints. We continue, stopping from time to time to look at tracks beside the road, or to question the occasional person we meet. Twenty-five kilometres later we arrive at the next village, Enkowit, and stop. The police inform the head of the village who says he'll spread the word to be on the lookout. We turn back. By the time we get close to Summit, it's almost sunset and visibility is falling off. We leave the road to the right, then drive parallel looking for tracks. Then we do the same to the left of the road. One of the policemen tells me we'll try again tomorrow. Then suddenly the jeep stops at some tracks. Everybody gets out to look at them. To me, camel tracks all look the same. But like a human fingerprint, every camel has its unique footprint. The tracker tells me these are mine. The jeep takes off after the tracks, to get as far as possible before dark slows us down. The thief is making slow progress. His footprints are in front of the camel's, pulling. He must have got a surprise to find out he'd stolen an exhausted camel. The jeep stops, and the guide gets on the hood to see better. We continue. Soon it's too dark and the jeep stops again. The guide gets off and starts alternating between jogging and walking. The jeep follows him closely with its headlights on, to give him as much light as possible. An hour later, the jeep stops at a big bush. The tracker shows me the marks where the thief rested. He picks up a piece of dung, and tells me it's quite fresh. They're excited now. They take out their guns. I look at one of them. "You won't shoot him, will you?" He just looks at me very strangely. He starts to jog beside the tracker, his pistol in his hand. At 8 p.m., we suddenly see a camel ahead in the headlights. He's hobbled and grazing. The jeep drives up to him and stops. I tell them he's mine. A policeman tells me to get out of the jeep with him. The jeep leaves to look for the thief. The policeman guarding me lies down on his stomach with his rifle and tells me to do the same. He doesn't want me standing in case there are shots. I watch the jeep's headlights move back and forth in the distance. Then they stop. The policeman stands up, and we take my camel with us to the jeep, which is stopped at the thief's camp. He's gone! When he spotted our headlights coming from the horizon, he knew who it was. He was so afraid, he ran away without taking his belongings. A tiny cup of coffee sits untouched on the sand. I feel it with my fingers. I'm relieved he got away. The coffee is warm. If not for the darkness, he wouldn't have been able to escape.

October 31
I get up at dawn, tired. I didn't get back to the police station to sleep until 1 a.m. last night. I hitchhike back to where I'd taken the track, after my camel was stolen two days ago. I don't explain to the police where I'm going. They wouldn't understand. Then I walk the four and a half kilometres back to the police station. I want to cover every inch across the Sahara myself.

My camel was already exhausted before he was stolen, and the distance and pace of the theft has made him worse. When I leave it's an effort for him to stand up. I don't even go to the Scandinavian aid organization to thank them: I'm too worried he might sit down there and not be able to get up. I send a message thanking them.

I walk seven and a half kilometres, leaving the railroad and following the road, until I find some grazing and stop. He going to get even more exhausted if I don't let him eat. In the afternoon, just as I'm leaving, a vehicle stops, and a policeman asks me for identification. Worried that my camel won't be able to stand up if I sit him down to get my Travel Permit from my bag, I climb up to get it. The policeman checks it and leaves. A minute later another policeman stops to ask me for identification. When he's finished, I ask him to help me get my camel up. As he pulls the reins I push as hard as I can from behind. My camel can't do it. We try again and again. Then they help me unload him and I camp. I start to wait until tomorrow, to try again.

Endnotes

N'Djamena, Chad
5 June 1990

Mr. Frank Cole
C/O Esso-Tchad
N'djamena, Chad

Dear Mr. Cole:

I am writing to record recent the conversations between
you and members of this embassy regarding your proposed
travel, alone, overland, and by camel, through Chad and
into Sudan.

As you will remember, we noted to you the unsettled
conditions in the Darfur region of Sudan through which
you intend to pass after you leave Chad. We described
the region as one in which Sudanese Governmental
authority was weak and where local conditions of public
order were uncertain. We called to your attention that
the very area you propose to traverse was recently the
scene of violent battles between the Chadian Army and
well-armed anti-Chadian rebels, and that we could not
rule out future similar violence in the area.

I therefore wish to repeat to you our considered
recommendation that you do not attempt to travel
through the Darfur region of Sudan alone and on
camelback, as you have proposed to do.

I wish you good luck in your future endeavors.

Sincerely,

Louis John Nigro
Consul

FAX: 996-5358 J. Carisse, Director Consular
                                Operations Division,
From: C. Cole. Ottawa, Tel.   M.F.A.
        737-6029   August 22, 2000
        SAHARA CAMEL TRIP- FRANK COLE
        SITUATION REPORT

Nothing has been heard from Frank Cole since he
left Nouakchott in early July in pursuance of his project to
travel across the Sahara Desert and neighbouring countries.
He had hoped to arrive in Nema in eastern Mauritania about
August 15. Before leaving Nouakchott he had indicated to
us by fax that he would decide enroute whether to travel
to Nema by way of Tidjikia or Kiffa. This decision was
influened by the Saharan drought and the dry water holes
experienced during his previous route in May and June and
which caused him to travel from Atar to Nouakchott to
begin a fresh start on the route indicated above. He is
travelling alone .with two camels and making a documentary film.

Frank had been in touch with Canadian Missions prior to
departure and we sent a brief situation report to them on
July 20 i.e. :

Dakar/C. Bernard   Ethiopia/ Miloff
Morocco/ Cousineau   Egypt/ Dunn
Mali/ Cliche
Niger/ Bigras   Also to MFA: Eastern & Southern
Cameroun/ Edwards   Africa Division/ Melvill
                                         Arts Promotion/ Rosebrugh

----

Frank had made a similar trip by camel alone across the
Sahara in 1989-90 when he made a documentary. He told us
before leaving that tracing him, if necessary, should be
facilitated by the fact that children and others in the
communities through which he passed turned out to see him.
His clothing is dark and he wears a wide-brimmed dark hat.

It would be appreciated if Canadian Missions could
be requested to ask diplomatic counterparts, particularly
the Americans and the British to let them know if they
have any information or learn anything relating to Frank's

present location and his immediate plans. How is his
health as well as that of his camels? We.realize, of
course. that any information at present would more
likely come to the attention of Missions proximate to
Frank's location.

Mr. Carisse: Many thanks. Could we be copied on your fax.

The e-mail of Frank's friend is ed182@ freenet. carleton.
ca   (Sonja Hrisic)

CRYONICS INSTITUTE
24355 Sorrentino Court
Clinton Township MI 48035
Phone (810) 791-5961, Phone/Fax (810) 792-7062, E-Mail <cryonics@cryonics.org>
http://www.cryonics.org

R.C.W. Ettinger
3326 N. 81 St.
Scottsdale AZ 85251
Phone (480) 941-5591, Fax (480) 947-7759, E-Mail <ettinger@aol.com>

Nov. 2, 2000

Sdttoibrain
613 7373734

Charles Cole
Via fax 613-737-2825.~~(Mail Boxes)~~

Dear Mr. Cole:

Referring to our recent phone conversation concerning sending your son's (Frank Cole's) body from Mali to CI (to arrive at Detroit Metropolitan Airport, either directly from Mali or from Ottawa):

Although his condition is extremely deteriorated, since you want to honor his wish to be cryopreserved regardless of condition, we will accept and cryopreserve him if he is sent to us, and assuming his life insurance policy for $100,000 Canadian will be paid to CI. We are also willing then to pay the estimated $16,500 for local expenses in Mali and transportation.

If the local people want prepayment of local expenses, I suggest you offer to give them half ahead of time and the balance upon receipt of Frank's body. CI is willing to help with prepayment of local expenses, if necessary, once the life insurance company verifies that the insurance is still in effect with CI as beneficiary and they will pay it upon receipt of proof of death in the form of a statement from the Canadian embassy in Mali.

As to the shipping container, there are no special requirements as far as we are concerned, except that a desiccant should be included to keep the body dry. (It is too late for temperature to make a difference.)

Once more, our deepest sympathy in your terrible loss.

Robert Ettinger, President
Cryonics Institute

A Documentary
8 minutes, black and white, 16mm, 1979
When François Truffault remarked that all directors are condemned to remake their first film again and again, he might have been naming the project of Frank Cole. In Frank's first short film, made at Algonquin College, he brings a terrifying mixture of intimacy and distance to bear on his aging grandparents. The camera is both stunned observer and an instrument of relentless pressure, urging its subject to go on, to show what cannot be seen.

Each frame is memorial, each shot might last forever. Each small moment of shoe-tying and hallway-walking is a necessary prelude to the film's closing moment, where Frank's grandmother lies in bed, hardly human, as close to death as one could be without giving in. Beside her is her lifelong partner, himself grown so very old, helplessly resigned to counting the remaining hours. In reaction to their failing flesh, the camera takes on the rigid architectural framings of the hospital, refusing any easy warmth and closeness, but maintaining always the terrible repression of distance, the merciless measurement required to look, and it is this calculus of pain that Frank revisits in movie after movie.

The camera squeezes the two grandparents; it pushes and pulls until it is clear that what we are watching is at once a couple at the end of their days, and death itself. It is as if, through the lens of his new medium, Cole is able to see his beloved grandparents for the first time, but the cost of his new-found seeing must be paid by his subject. The ones he loved beyond death.

The Mountenays
22 minutes, black and white, 16mm, 1981
Frank's second movie was also made at Algonquin College. It is a short black-and-white marvel of direct cinema. Here he visits the Mountenay family who live in a stretch of abandoned forest, next to an auto junkyard in the Ottawa Valley. The brothers appear first in a nearly endless succession, and even though it is winter they are busy out of doors for most of the day, tapping trees for maple syrup, but more usually spilling out of car hulks that they work to resuscitate. They hurtle past the lens on skis or cars or sleighs, laughing and falling over and having a good-old-boy time. No one is getting dressed for work or school or bending over seedlings or getting framed up into architectures reserved for growing up or getting old. They look feral, as wild as the animals that are roosting around coops that don't seem much different than the big old house they all live inside. How

many of them are there? Twenty-odd, maybe more. Frank talks to them behind his camera shield, asking good-humoured questions that sound like straight-man chatter from one of the Apollo missions. They eat it up, of course. They call him Frankie, they put it on a little bit, but always there is life happening while the camera rolls. An Elvis song is struck up and down, and there is a summons for dinner, all those faces pooling in the natural light, asking, "What next?"

In the end they gather for a family portrait out of doors, the boys and girls and young ones and mother calling out for those still tending to some off-screen moment while the camera keeps on rolling. There is nothing frozen or stillborn or lost, no summary glance. Perhaps in the end there is nothing to add up, only another glimpse into a home life, parts of the long home movie that Frank was busy making whenever he turned on the camera.

A Life
75 minutes, black and white, 16mm, 1986
Vito Acconci, Joan Jonas, Chris Burden ... Frank Cole? Yes, with this movie Frank comes out as a performance artist extraordinaire. His body, like theirs, is a machine for producing pictures.

Frank's nearly wordless solo performance for camera finds him back-and-forthing between a horizonless Sahara and a room that contains only a desk and a bed. His double life is insistently crosscut in rhyming movements, as if he were in two places at once. Every moment is choreographed and rehearsed, so what we are seeing is never the thing itself, but instead an echo or double of that moment. Even when we are seeing a simple action like lighting a match or walking across a room, we are watching a performance of that action, instead of the action itself. A set of architectural drawings maps out his room and the gestural vocabulary it might contain, a scored choreography that anticipates movements that never occur for the first time.

In the desert, ground swallows figure again and again. This reconfiguration of foreground and background becomes, in Frank's cosmology, a consideration of life and death. Death is the ground against which we cast our shadows, every sandy footfall a temporary intrusion. When a vial of his grandfather's ashes breaks in Frank's room, he sweeps it up and eats it. But in the desert it is the merely human who is swept from one dune to the next, overtaken and digested.

Joseph Beuys famously performed with a wild coyote in *Coyote: I Love America and America Loves Me* (1974). For a week Beuys lived in an art-gallery cage with an untrained animal, wrapped in felt whenever necessary to ward off unwanted attentions. Beuys had his coyote, Frank his snake. The large reptile slithers across his bed and floor, where he takes hold of it and then releases it, confronting it again and again. Finally he becomes the snake, emerging as a slithering mass across the desert and then the floor of his room, smeared in blood.

Life Without Death
83 minutes, black and white, 16mm, 2000

Life Without Death appears as a sequel or extended coda to *A Life*. Once more the film opens with an image of Cole's beloved grandfather, Frank Howard, whose absence requires another penitential voyage across the Sahara. Before the death of his grandparents, there was no need to produce doubles of the world, but once the wound is open the pictures flow in an attempt to cover what is missing. The wrapping, the bandage, the stanchion: it's never enough.

While *A Life* issues a combination of landscape and performance art, *Life Without Death* is a distinctly linear travelogue narrative of crossing the Sahara, accompanied by voice-over narration. The story Cole relates is simple enough: the search for water, the desertion of his guides, getting lost, the struggle with fear and loneliness.

The cinematography is precise and rendered always in the first person, offering picture-perfect landscapes from the solidity of three legs or else a lilting view on top of a camel. Impossibly, owing to his largely solitary travel, Cole shoots his voyaging with a wind-up camera and a timer, so that he can step in front of the lens and perform himself. There are periodic returns throughout his trek to moments that might be outtakes from his first film, showing his grandfather looking out a window, or lying in bed. Again and again these two figures are married via montage, one gesture rhyming another. Frank lies down and his grandfather likewise; they are finding their home together in the world of pictures.

In the end, having crossed the Sahara, he kneels beside his camel as they look out at their Red Sea destination. Frank says, "Alive." It was the last word he would ever speak on film.

A Documentary, The Mountenays
and *A Life*:
Canadian Film Institute
2 Daly Avenue, Suite 120
Ottawa, Ontario, K1N 6E2
613.232.6727
info@cfi-icf.ca
www.cfi-icf.ca

Life Without Death:
Necessary Illusions Productions Inc.
24 avenue du Mont-Royal Ouest
Montréal, QC, Canada H2T 2S2
514.287.7337
info@necessaryillusions.ca
www.necessaryillusions.ca

The Man Who Crossed the Sahara
a documentary by Korbett Matthews

53 minutes, 16mm, 2008

In his latest documentary, the poetic lens of Korbett Matthews channels the ghost of deceased Canadian filmmaker Frank Cole. Shot with some of the same stark beauty that impelled Cole's death-defying movies, Matthews brings us home with Cole's family and close-up with the cameraman he dragged across the Sahara. He swims alongside best friend Rick Taylor, and then brings us to filmmaker and wordsmith Peter Wintonick (*Manufacturing Consent*). Each provides a fascinating, haunting glimpse into the single-minded burn that drove Cole into the *Guinness Book of World Records* as the only person to cross the Sahara alone.

The Man Who Crossed the Sahara is a movie generous with inner and outer geographies. Not only does it travel back to Cole's terminal point in Mali, it brings us to the Cryonics Institute outside Detroit where his remains lie in a state of deep-freeze preservation. These travels are accompanied by Richard Horowitz's (*The Sheltering Sky*) pan-African score and Kara Blake's winning photo animations. We are offered, above all, an approach to these outsider pictures and journeys, a way inside a body dedicated to a relentless vigil against death. This murder mystery teems with a tender and infernal beauty.

I plan to travel to the place where you were buried by Tuareg nomads. Of this, you have no memory. I will retrace your last few days alive and seek to make sense of what happened to you out there that day. Was it morning or night? I will attempt to finish the film that you were interrupted from completing. To bring closure to your life. To find the people of the sands who remember you. To find your camera, your film. To perhaps find those who took your life. I will interview the Sahara, the sole witness of the crime, to come closer to understanding you, the man in the photograph whom I never met. This film is a gift for you, a time capsule. A gift that will be placed next to you in Michigan, in case you ever awaken. — Korbett Matthews

Contributors

Yann Beauvais is one of the foremost experimental film/video artists of France. Besides producing a considerable body of work in film and video, intimately linking the formal and the political, Beauvais has written widely on film, curated numerous programs worldwide and founded Light Cone distribution and Scratch Projection in Paris. He lives and works in Paris and São Paulo and teaches at the École des Arts in Mulhouse.

Mike Cartmell is a Canadian media artist currently in Ithaca. He has contributed notable texts on alternative media, including the title essay for a collection of writings on Phil Hoffman called *Landscape with Shipwreck*.

Lisa Cole worked several years as a licenced projectionist at the Vogue Cinema in Sackville, N.B., before completing her degree in English Literature and Creative Writing at the University of New Brunswick. She is now a freelance writer, editor and web designer living in Victoria, B.C. Her short script *Katalina and the Elf*, a fable about two girls growing up in P.E.I., is currently in post-production.

John Greyson is a Toronto film/video artist whose shorts, features and installations include *Fig Trees* (2003, Oakville Art Galleries); *Proteus* (Best Actor, Sithenghi 2003); *The Law of Enclosures* (2000, Best Actor Genie); *Lilies* (1996, Best Film Genie, Best Film at festivals in Montreal, Johannesburg, Los Angeles, San Francisco); *Un©ut* (1997, Honourable Mention, Berlin Film Festival); *Zero Patience* (1993, Best Canadian Film, Sudbury Film Festival); *The Making of Monsters* (1991, Best Canadian Short, Toronto Film Festival; Best Short Film Teddy, Berlin Film Festival); and *Urinal* (1988, Best Feature Teddy, Berlin Film Festival). He co-edited *Queer Looks*, a critical anthology on gay/lesbian film and video (Routledge, 1993), is the author of *Urinal and Other Stories* (Power Plant/Art Metropole, 1993) and has published essays and artist's pieces in *Alphabet City*, *Public*, *Fuse* and twelve critical anthologies. An assistant professor in film production at York University, he was awarded the Toronto Arts Award for Film/Video, 2000, and the Bell Canada Video Art Award in 2007.

Mike Hoolboom has published two books of interviews with Canadian movie artists, *Inside the Pleasure Dome* (2000) and *Practical Dreamers* (2008). He continues to work on a large internet database project for Canadian media artists that can be found at www.fringeonline.ca.

Greg Klymkiw has devoted his life and career to the development, distribution and production of indigenous, independent Canadian film culture. He has written and/or produced numerous award-winning and critically acclaimed films, marketed the work of the legendary Winnipeg Film Group, written on film and popular culture for print, radio and television, taught many courses and workshops, and delivered guest lectures on filmmaking in a multitude of venues and institutions worldwide. He is currently the Producer-in-Residence at the Canadian Film Centre, where he is firmly committed to the training and development of the next generation of Canada's filmmakers.

Deirdre Logue has spent the past eighteen years working on behalf of media artists by organizing independent film, video and new-media festivals and by participating in forums and symposiums on the future of independent artistic production and film and video distribution. She was a founding member of Media City in Windsor, the executive director of the Images Festival of Independent Film and Video from 1995 to 1999, the executive director at the Canadian Filmmakers Distribution Centre from 2001 to 2006 and is currently the development director for Vtape.

Korbett Matthews is a Montreal-based documentary filmmaker whose work has been awarded prizes by such festivals as the Images Festival, Docupolis, the Yorkton Short Film Festival, LAlterniva Festival of Independent Cinema, the Amnesty International Film Festival and Hot Docs Canadian International Documentary Film Festival. In 2005 he opened 7th Embassy, his own film production company, and he is currently working on *The India Space Opera*, a visual documentary set thirty years in the future when India sends a man into space, and *Farewell to Grozny*, a poetic exploration of the Chechen conflict, a war long forgotten by the West. He obtained his MFA in Film Production from Concordia University's Mel Hoppenheim School of Cinema after working for five years on *The Man Who Crossed the Sahara*, a documentary about Frank Cole. He currently works as a lecturer in media arts at Breda University in the Netherlands.

Tom McSorley is the director of the Canadian Film Institute and a sessional lecturer in Film Studies at Carleton University in Ottawa. A freelance film critic for CBC Radio One and contributor to various Canadian and international cinema publications, he is also the editor of *Rivers of Time* (2008), which examines the work of Phil Hoffman, and is the co-editor of *Self Portraits: The*

Cinemas of Canada Since Telefilm (2006). His book-length study of Atom Egoyan's *The Adjuster* is forthcoming.

Peter Mettler is known for a diversity of work in image and sound mediums — foremost for his films such as *Picture of Light* and *Gambling, Gods and LSD,* but also as a photographer and live audio/visual mixing performer. His work melds experimental, narrative, personal essay and documentary forms around notions of perception and consciousness. He has collaborated with an extensive range of international artists and has been honoured with awards and retrospectives worldwide. A book on his work entitled *Making the Invisible Visible* was published in 1995 and another entitled *Of This Place and Elsewhere, The Films and Photography of Peter Mettler* was published in 2006 by the Toronto International Film Festival.

Laurie Monsebraaten has been a reporter for the *Toronto Star* since 1983. During this time, she has covered general news, Toronto City Hall and the social-policy beat. She has also been an editorial writer and member of the weekend features team. Her work has been nominated twice for the Michener Award for Public Service Journalism and numerous times for National Newspaper Awards. She was born and raised in Ottawa and holds an Honours Degree in Journalism from Carleton University. She lives in Toronto with her husband and two children.

Julie Murray was born in Dublin, Ireland. She has completed more than twenty short films and has collaborated on many film installation/performance events with artists, musicians and other filmmakers. Along with numerous screenings at the Museum of Modern Art, the Whitney Museum of American Art, New York, S F Cinematheque and the Pacific Film Archive in California, Murray has been invited to present her films at the Art Gallery of Ontario, Toronto; Anthology Film Archives, New York; Hallwalls, Buffalo, NY; Film Forum, LA; and at various universities.

Fred Pelon is an artist-filmmaker working in Amsterdam. A notorious internationalist and streetfighter turned into a Buddhist meditator teaching insight meditation. His award-winning movies have toured the globe.

Born in Paris in 1952, **Jean Perret** attended schools and university in Zurich and Geneva. His master's thesis in contemporary history was dedicated to Swiss documentaries of the 1930s. Since then, he has written many articles for newspapers, magazines, books. He has taught semiotics and cinema, worked for the public radio and has produced television broadcasts for independent documentaries. In charge of the documentary section at the Festival of Locarno, in 1995 he became the director of the International Film Festival of Nyon, "Visions du Réel."

Geoff Pevere worked as the Canadian programmer for Toronto's Festival of Festivals (where he programmed Frank's *A Life*), is the best-selling author of *Mondo Canuck*, has been the film reviewer for the *Toronto Star* for the past two decades and has recently switched to writing about books. He hails from Ottawa, where he met Frank and wrote an early review of *The Mountenays*.

Steve Reinke is an artist and writer best known for his work in video. He lives in Toronto and Chicago, where he is associate professor of Art Theory and Practice at Northwestern. His recent books include *Everybody Loves Nothing: Video 1996–2004* (Coach House) and the anthology *The Sharpest Point: Animation at the End of Cinema* (edited with Chris Gehman; YYZ Books).

Richard Taylor is the author of the novel *Cartoon Woods*, the short-story collection *Tender Only to One* and a travel memoir, *House Inside the Waves: Domesticity, Art and the Surfing Life*. Many of his feature articles, on subjects as diverse as Lord Byron, open-water swimming, surfing, hiking, and the perils and pleasures of being a househusband, have been published in magazines and literary quarterlies. A seasoned traveller, he has journeyed around the world twice and has taught writing in Hong Kong, Australia and Tuscany. Today he teaches writing at Algonquin College, Ottawa, and since he was hired as writer in residence in 1995, he has taught the fiction workshop and lectured in twentieth-century literature at Carleton University, Ottawa. Because he has trolled his toes in the seven seas, at present he is writing an unusual book about swimming with writers called *Water and Desire*.

Ben Vandoorne was born in Brussels, Belgium, in 1968. He lived in Luxor, Egypt, for seven years, where he worked in tourism as a guide and an independent organizer of adventure tours. It was during this time that he made his first amateur films. He has made one feature film, *Incha Allah*, shot in the Sahara, and now works solely on films.

'Frank Cole's *A Life*' by Greg Klymkiw was originally published in *Cinema Canada*, March 1989.
Candid Camera' by Frank Cole was originally published in *Cinema Canada*, March 1989)

Edited by Mike Hoolboom and Tom McSorley
Designed by Alana Wilcox

Photo credits:
Pages 4, 8, 9, 12, 13, 15, 193, 195, 196 and 197, courtesy of the Cole Family
Page 21 and all colour postcards, courtesy of Richard Taylor
Page 23 (bottom), Dale Taylor
Page 31, Anne Milligan
Page 96, courtesy of the Colin Campbell estate
All other pictures by Frank Cole.

The enclosed DVD contains *The Man Who Crossed the Sahara*, a documentary by Korbett Matthews.

The editors would like to thank Charles Cole, Peter Cole, Rick/Simon, Tina Legari, Keeley Durocher, Dan Sokolowski, Jennifer Noseworthy, Scott Birdwise, Kelly Friesen, Sam Kula, Richard Lochead, Colin Browne, Kelly Langgard, David Novek, Peter Wintonick.

Canadian Film Institute
2 Daly Avenue, Suite 120
Ottawa, Ontario K1N 6E2
T 613.232.6727   F 613.232.6315
info@cfi-icf.ca   www.cfi-icf.ca

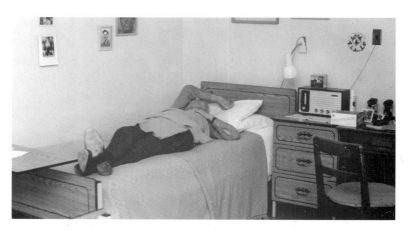

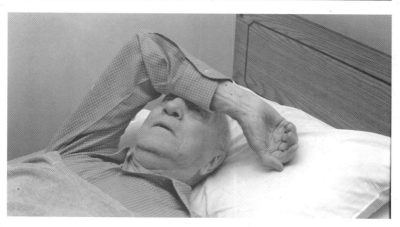